Fw 190 *STURMBÖCKE*
VS
B-17 FLYING FORTRESS
Europe 1944–45

ROBERT FORSYTH

First published in Great Britain in 2009 by Osprey Publishing,
Midland House, West Way, Botley, Oxford, OX2 0PH, UK
443 Park Avenue South, New York, NY 10016, USA
E-mail: info@ospreypublishing.com

A CIP catalog record for this book is available from the British Library

Print ISBN: 978 1 84603 941 6
PDF e-book ISBN: 978 184603 942 3

Page layout by: Ken Vail Graphic Design, Cambridge, UK
Index by Alison Worthington
Typeset in ITC Conduit and Adobe Garamond
Maps by Bounford.com, Cambridge, UK
Originated by PDQ Digital Media Solutions, Suffolk, UK
Printed in China through Bookbuilders

09 10 11 12 13   10 9 8 7 6 5 4 3 2 1

FOR A CATALOG OF ALL BOOKS PUBLISHED BY OSPREY MIL-
ITARY AND AVIATION PLEASE CONTACT:

Osprey Direct, c/o Random House Distribution Center,
400 Hahn Road, Westminster, MD 21157
Email: uscustomerservice@ospreypublishing.com

Osprey Direct, The Book Service Ltd, Distribution Centre,
Colchester Road, Frating Green, Colchester, Essex, CO7 7DW
E-mail: customerservice@ospreypublishing.com

www.ospreypublishing.com

Dedication
This book is dedicated to the memory of Ian Nisbet "Wilco"
Wilcockson. Countryman, sportsman, soldier, businessman,
bon viveur and friend to many.

Fw 190 cover art
Flying his Fw 190A-8/R2, Wk-Nr 681385 "White 16",
Oberfähnrich Franz Schaar of 5.(*Sturm*)/JG 4 closes in to attack
B-17Gs of the US 3rd Bomb Division (BD) over Magdeburg
on the morning of Tuesday, September 12, 1944. The Eighth Air
Force had despatched a force of nearly 900 bombers to strike at
synthetic fuel plants and refinery targets across central Germany on
this date. In a typical *Sturmgruppe* assault, Schaar had already made
one firing pass with the rest of his *Gruppen*, and he is depicted here
having fought his way through the American fighter escort for
a second pass, together with Unteroffizier Herbert Chlond also
of 5.(*Sturm*)/JG 4. Each pilot would inflict sufficent damage on
a B-17 to force it out of formation, thus leaving it as a "straggler"
– a lone, vulnerable bomber without protection, almost certain to
attract a further, probably fatal, attack. This mission represented
Schaar's second aerial success. (Artwork by Gareth Hector)

B-17 Flying Fortress cover art
The crew of B-17G 42-31924 *Ol' Dog* of the 344th BS/95th BG
desperately attempt to defend themselves against an attack by
Fw 190s of IV./JG 3 during their mission to bomb aircraft plants
at Leipzig on May 29, 1944. 2Lt Norman A. Ulrich's crew was to
endure a draining ordeal, the pilot recalling "Over the intercom I
heard 'Fighters at ten o'clock', and when I looked out the window,
I could see them in front of us. They were coming at us, and fast!
Within seconds of this sighting, the world exploded and total
monotony became total terror. I remember two Fw 190s coming
at us, but one in particular seemed to have us in his sights with his
cannon blazing away. I could feel the impact of his shells hitting
our airplane, but at the same time I saw the Fw 190 getting hits
and a large piece of it falling off." As if that was not enough, *Ol'
Dog* would suffer further close-range head-on and beam attacks
by Fw 190s of IV./JG 3 as it endeavored to make its way home
as a lone "straggler". The aircraft eventually crash-landed and its
crew survived as prisoners of war. (Artwork by Gareth Hector)

Acknowledgements
The author would like to thank the following who have kindly
assisted him with information, documents and photographs (some
many years ago, others much more recently) – Oscar Boesch,
Eddie J. Creek, Keith Ferris, Mark Forlow, Richard Franz, Eric
Mombeek, Gary L. Moncur (for more information on the
303rd BG visit www.303rdbg.com), Lt Col Harry D. Gobrecht,
USAF(Ret), Donald Nijboer, Mark Postlethwaite, Barry Smith
and Willi Unger.

CONTENTS

INTRODUCTION

During the Great Depression of the early 1930s, less than ten years before America entered the war against Germany, a sense of ultimate faith, fostered by a clique of officers at the US Army Air Corps Tactical School (ACTS) at Maxwell Field, Alabama, slowly but surely formed around the apparent invincibility and capabilities of the heavy bomber as a weapon of strategic offense. This faith eventually emerged as doctrine.

The root of this doctrine, and the cause of so much faith in the heavy bomber, has been attributed to a great extent to the hypothesis espoused by the (at the time) little-known Italian air power theorist, Guilio Douhet. He prophesied the brilliant and conquering future of the aerial bomber, derived from his personal experiences during Italy's war against the Turks in 1911.

Translated into English by 1921, Douhet's controversial theories were to transform military aviation doctrines around the globe, and many came to believe slavishly in the coming age of air power, envisaging fleets of high-flying bombers so well-armed that they would fend off – and even destroy – an enemy's disorganized and outnumbered fighter forces.

American writers opined that bombers would be used in mass over urban centers, their vast numbers darkening the sky as they went about destroying factories with such pinpoint accuracy that terrorized citizens of major cities would be left all too ready to surrender under a rain of falling bombs. Indeed, artists painted scenes of an enemy's sky dotted with Army Air Corps bombers dropping endless sticks of bombs upon defenseless factories. Enemy fighters were depicted firing harmlessly from out of range, or spinning down in flames as victims of the bombers' "fortress-like" armament. It was of course total fantasy, but this view was not without its advocates. Even across the Atlantic, the British Conservative politician Stanley Baldwin stated in late 1932 that "No power on earth can protect the man in the street from being bombed. Whatever people may tell him, the bomber will always get through."

Certainly, the advocates at the ACTS espoused the virtues of bomber technology over the further development of "pursuit" or fighter interceptor aviation. In 1934, for example, Capts Harold L. George and Robert M. Webster of the ACTS carried out an in-depth analysis of the vulnerability of New York City to daylight precision bombing. Both officers came to the conclusion that if bombs could be used to accurately strike essential services – i.e. water, electricity and transportation – the effect would be to make the city "unliveable".

George's, Webster's and many other officers' faith in the heavy bomber was strengthened drastically when, in July 1935, Boeing produced its four-engined, highly streamlined, all-metal Model 299 to conform to an ambitious Army Air Corps requirement for a long-range maritime patrol bomber to protect the extensive US coastline.

It had been Brig Gen William M. "Billy" Mitchell, one time Assistant Chief of the Air Service, who had warned that the development of the long-range military aircraft fundamentally changed the defensive position of the United States. "Aircraft will project the spearpoint of the nation's offensive and defensive power against the vital centres of the opposing country", he forecast. "The result of warfare by air will be to bring about quick decisions. Superior air power will cause such havoc, or the threat of such havoc, in the opposing country that a long drawn out campaign will be impossible. Woe be to the nation that is weak in the air."

The aircraft's ability to travel much farther and faster than previous means of transportation removed the isolation the USA had previously counted on as part of its security.

Based on a commercial airliner design and enjoying a program of continued further development, the 100ft-wingspan Model 299 was powered by four 750hp Pratt & Whitney R-1690-E Hornet nine-cylinder air-cooled radial engines, and featured four blister-type flexible machine gun stations, each of which could accommodate a 0.30in. or 0.50in machine gun. An additional station for a nose machine gun was incorporated, and a bomb load of up to eight 600lb bombs could be carried internally.

It is popularly believed that upon observing the aircraft on its maiden flight at Seattle on July 28, 1935, one impressed newspaper reporter from the *Seattle Daily Times* commented that it had the appearance of a "flying fortress". Equally, the officers at the ACTS were convinced about the impregnability of what eventually became the B-17 Flying Fortress.

However, by the late 1930s any euphoria over the fledgling B-17 ignored the fact that the advent of radar technology and high-performance fighters wholly undermined Douhet's theory that bombers would always "get through". Furthermore, allegiance to the Douhet doctrine ignored the possibility that an enemy's defenses would be developed at all. Indeed, the destruction of the Luftwaffe did not become the main priority of the Anglo-American strategic bombing campaign until the launch of Operation *Pointblank* in 1943.

Clad in typical period flight gear, crew members of a B-17 Flying Fortress hitch a ride out to their aircraft on bomb and ammunition trailers at an Eighth Air Force base somewhere in England in early 1943. The B-17 in the background carries an early-style fuselage star, and the top turret aft of the cockpit with its twin Browning machine guns is clearly visible. The officer in the foreground is sitting on a 2,000lb bomb, but he does not appear to be unduly perturbed!

Before that, however, from the time the United States Army Air Force (USAAF) despatched its B-17s to England in mid-1942 to equip the heavy bomber groups of the Eighth Air Force, their crews quickly began to learn the hard way.

Across the English Channel, and following the experience of nearly three years of fighting the Polish, French, Dutch, Belgian, British and Soviet air forces, the Luftwaffe had honed a sophisticated air defense network in occupied Western Europe. By mid-June 1942, the Jagdwaffe fielded a force of nearly 160 Messerschmitt Bf 109F fighters in the West. This aircraft had proved itself to be a worthy opponent to the Royal Air Force (RAF) during the Channel battles and "Circuses", "Rhubarbs" and "Rodeos" of 1941, with pilots such as Leutnant Egon Mayer of 7./JG 2 and Oberleutnant Josef Priller, the *Staffelkapitän* of 1./JG 26, representative of the growing number of German pilots attaining high individual scores against the British Spitfires. The RAF realized it faced a formidable foe that was not going to buckle.

But even more formidable and ominous was the appearance in late 1941 of a new German fighter in the skies over France – the pugnacious, radial-engined Focke-Wulf Fw 190. Entering service with JGs 2 and 26, the aircraft was powered by a BMW 801, the D variant of which developed 1,700hp. Despite initial technical problems with the engine, as well as with the ailerons, elevators and undercarriage on the early A-1 and A-2 variants, the Fw 190 soon proved itself to be a dependable fighter aircraft. Above 6,000m, it was markedly superior to the Spitfire V and

Hurricane II, and armed with two nose-mounted 7.92mm MG 17 machine guns, two fast-firing MG 151/20 cannon in the wings positioned close to the wing roots, and with provision for two 20mm MG FF cannon in the outer wings, it "packed a punch".

This considerable armament package blended with manoeuvrability on the ground, which pleased pilots. Indeed, the wide undercarriage track of the Fw 190 was vastly superior to the landing gear fitted to the Bf 109F, as was the air-cooled engine technology which bettered that of the more vulnerable liquid-cooled system on the Messerschmitt.

By June 20, 1942, *Luftflotte* 3 reported that it had some 250 Fw 190s on strength with II./JG 1, I., II. and III./JG 2 and I., II. and III./JG 26.

This came as a shock to the Allies, and it provided a new dimension to air combat on the Western Front – as did the appearance in strength of the USAAF's heavy bombers. The encounters which would follow between the B-17 and the Fw 190 over the next three years would form some of the most titanic and bitter contests of the air war in Western Europe.

An Fw 190A-7 of I./JG 11 is refuelled and rearmed at Rotenburg in March 1944. The armorers working below the wing are loading ammunition into the outer MG 151/20E wing-mounted cannon. The aircraft also carries a 300-liter drop tank. The A-7 variant packed a far heavier punch than the original Fw 190A-1 and A-2 of 1941–42, thus making it an ideal "bomber killer".

CHRONOLOGY

1935
July 28   Boeing Model 299 makes maiden flight in Seattle.

1937
January   First YB-17 "Flying Fortress" delivered to Wright Field.
September   *Reichsluftfahrtministerium* issues specification to Focke-Wulf for a fighter with performance superior to that of the Bf 109.

1938
July 18   Focke-Wulf issues drawing for first prototype of Fw 190 (the V1).

1939
June 1   Fw 190 V1 makes maiden flight in Bremen.

1941
May   Series production of Fw 190A-1 commences.
September   First deliveries of B-17E to United States Army Air Corps (USAAC).

1942
July 1   First B-17 of Eighth Air Force's VIII Bomber Command lands in UK.

August 17   First raid by USAAF heavy bombers against Continental target made when 12 B-17s of 97th BG attack marshalling yards at Rouen. No casualties.

1943
September   B-17G reaches Eighth Air Force units in England, fitted with chin turret for defense against Luftwaffe head-on attacks and enclosed waist gun positions.
October   *Sturmstaffel* 1 formed at Achmer with heavily armed and armored Fw 190A-7s and A-8s to counter increasing USAAF heavy bomber raids.
October 14 USAAF attacks Schweinfurt with 229 B-17s, of which 60 are lost, 17 seriously damaged and 121 damaged but repairable.

Groundcrews of the 97th BG wave as one of their group's B-17Es thunders overhead, probably at Grafton Underwood, in the summer of 1942. The 97th BG would launch the Eighth Air Force's bombing campaign in Europe when it attacked marshalling yards in northern France in August of that year. The aircraft seen here carries the pre-war US Army identification marking on the undersides of its wings.

November	Series production of Fw 190A-7 commences. MK 108 30mm cannon introduced.

1944

February	Fw 190A-8/R2 *Sturmflugzeug* production commences
March 6	*Sturmgruppen* engage 112 B-17s over Berlin. Fw 190s of *Sturmstaffel* 1 and IV./JG 3 claim more than 20 B-17s shot down.
April 13	Eighth Air Force extends bombing operations using B-17s to attack German aircraft manufacturing facilities in southern Germany.
May 8	Formation of IV.(*Sturm*)/JG 3.
July 7	First deployment of massed *Sturmgruppen* against US bombers during raid on oil and industrial targets in central Germany.
August 1	II.(*Sturm*)/JG 4 formed with Fw 190A-8s under Oberstleutnant von Kornatzki.
August 9	II./JG 300 redesignated as a *Sturmgruppe* with Fw 190A-8s under Major Dahl.
September 28	Massed attack by all *Sturmgruppen* against Eighth Air Force B-17s bombing Magdeburg. IV.(*Sturm*)/JG 3 account for ten of the 34 heavy bombers lost.
November 2	IV.(*Sturm*)/JG 3 claim 21 B-17s destroyed, but lose 21 Fw 190s in the process.
December 2	IV.(*Sturm*)/JG 3 make the last major *Sturm* assault of the war, claiming 22 heavy bombers destroyed southwest of Koblenz.

Major Walther Dahl, *Kommodore* of JG 300, admires the celebratory decoration applied to the spinner of his Fw 190A-8 "Blue 13" at Finsterwalde in September 1944 following the occasion of his 75th victory – a B-17G Flying Fortress shot down over Halle-Leipzig on the morning of the 11th.

DESIGN AND DEVELOPMENT

Fw 190A

Arguably, the Focke-Wulf Fw 190 evolved into wartime Germany's most effective fighter, offering the Luftwaffe the benefit of manoeuvrability combined with stability as a formidable gun platform and the flexibility to perform as an air superiority fighter, a heavily armed and armored interceptor and as an ordnance-carrying ground-attack aircraft.

Yet the development of the Fw 190 was often protracted and tortuous. Following a specification by the *Technisches Amt* (Technical Office) of the *Reichsluftfahrtministerium* (RLM) in 1937 to Focke-Wulf Flugzeugbau GmbH for a fighter with a performance that would be superior to that of the still new and largely untested Bf 109, the firm's Technical Director, Dipl.-Ing. Kurt Tank, and his design team at Bremen dutifully turned to the drawing board.

However, before the first project drawings were issued there were voices of discontent – not from Messerschmitt or other manufacturers, but from within the RLM itself. There were those who considered the Bf 109 to be of such advanced design that it would be impossible to develop and construct another fighter of comparable performance and quality. In any case, claimed the dissenters, any future war involving German arms would not last long enough to justify the time and expense of its development, or to find the aircraft sufficient employment. Furthermore, Focke-Wulf's response was to think in terms of a rugged aircraft built first and foremost for *interception*, and therefore able to absorb considerable punishment in action, not specifically for *offense* or *attack*. This philosophy won little support in the corridors of the RLM.

German air doctrine at this stage envisioned a short war – weeks or months at the most, with an enemy defeated by swift movement and overwhelming force – and debate coursed through the RLM as to the Focke-Wulf proposal. Many believed that there would be no requirement for an aircraft whose *raison d'être* was essentially that of *defense*, let alone one which incorporated apparently highly dubious, heavy and expensive radial engine technology in preference to a more aerodynamically favorable inline, liquid-cooled engine.

However, Tank, a decorated war veteran, and Focke-Wulf's resolute and exceptionally gifted designer, remained undaunted, and within some quarters of the *Technisches Amt* he found support. Because an air-cooled radial was capable of withstanding more combat stress, and because Tank's design would not impinge upon production of the liquid-cooled DB 601 (the powerplant of the Bf 109), the RLM eventually relented and permitted the Focke-Wulf design to proceed.

In the summer of 1938 the RLM issued a contract for construction of three prototypes of the "Fw 190" – a single-seat fighter to be powered by the 18-cylinder, 1,550hp BMW 139 radial engine. Maintaining the tradition of naming its machines after birds, Focke-Wulf came to know the Fw 190 as the *"Würger"* ("Shrike"). Company drawings of the V1 dating from the autumn of 1938 show proposals to install an armament of two 7.9mm MG 17 and two 13mm MG 131 machine guns, all wing-mounted.

Focke-Wulf took its time and made strenuous efforts to ensure that structure and build were second to none, and that the design would demand the minimum of maintenance in operational conditions. Early on it was realized that the BMW 139 was suffering from teething problems, and it would ultimately prove to be the main fault in an otherwise beautiful and exemplary prototype by the time the unarmed Fw 190 V1 took to air for the first time on June 1, 1939. Indeed, Focke-Wulf's chief test pilot, Hans Sander, was nearly suffocated by exhaust fumes from an overheating engine that reached a temperature of more than 130° F during the flight.

BMW quickly offered a replacement in the form of the BMW 801, which was another radial engine of the same diameter, but longer and heavier by 159kg. This necessitated moving the cockpit further back and generally strengthening the airframe, which helped somewhat to alleviate the problem. However, Luftwaffe engineers noted that the whole project would hinge on the performance of the 1,600hp BMW 801. Problems still occurred with the new powerplant too, and in the case of the armed V6, the engine temperature soared to the extent that the ammunition in the cowl machine guns became dangerously hot during test-flying.

Focke-Wulf was fortunate in that no less a figure than Reichsmarschall Hermann Göring happened to be present when the BMW 801C-0-equipped fifth prototype flew with a reworked fuselage from Bremen in April 1940. It quickly became evident that the alterations to the design adversely affected wing loading, and thus manoeuvrability, but Göring apparently viewed the new aircraft with enthusiasm. Indeed, his endorsement provided the catalyst for the further production of a series of six Fw 190A-0s, and these were delivered to the test unit *Erprobungsstaffel* 190, commanded by Oberleutnant Otto Behrens, at Rechlin in late February 1941.

Difficulties were initially encountered with these machines. Occasionally the propeller mechanism proved troublesome, but it was the BMW 801C that caused the most headaches. Between the arrival of the Fw 190A-0s and the early summer, Behrens, a trained motor mechanic, and his engineers and pilots (most of the latter seconded from II./JG 26) undertook intensive trouble-shooting. Finally, by August 1941, things were deemed safe enough to allow the first Fw 190A-1 production machines, each armed with four Rheinmetall-Borsig MG 17s (two in the cowl and two in the wing roots) and two 20mm Oerlikon MG FF cannon in the outer wings, to be handed over to 6./JG 26 in Belgium. The new fighters replaced the *Staffel's* tried and tested Bf 109Es.

Unfortunately, despite the best efforts of *Erprobungsstaffel* 190, problems persisted – nine Fw 190s crashed between August and September, and according to Behrens' reports, the finger of blame was pointed at BMW, whose engines continued to be plagued by overheating and compressor damage. To make matters worse, there were further delays in deliveries associated with failings afflicting the anticipated 801D.

The Fw 190 was first blooded on September 18, 1941, when the *Gruppen-kommandeur* of II./JG 26, Spanish Civil War veteran and 25-victory Knight's Cross-holder Hauptmann Walter Adolph, was lost during a shipping escort mission off the Belgian coast following an encounter with RAF Blenheim IVs and Spitfires. This would mark the beginning of a series of early "spats" between Fw 190A-1s and Spitfire Vs that would last until the end of the year.

In late 1941 deliveries of the Fw 190A-2 to Major Gerhard Schöpfel's *Stab* JG 26 at Audembert and Major Johannes Seifert's I./JG 26 at St Omer commenced, this time in greater numbers than the A-1 since Focke-Wulf was supplemented in its output from Bremen by sub-contractors, Ago in Oschersleben and Arado at Warnemünde.

The A-2 benefited from an improved 1,600hp BMW 801C-2 that was cooled by extra ventilation slots at the rear of the engine. The aircraft also featured an uprated weapons array that included two 20mm Mauser MG 151 cannon built into the wing roots, with interrupter gear incorporated to allow synchronized fire through the propeller arc. The aircraft was fitted with a Revi C/12D reflector gunsight, FuG 7

Fw 190A-8/R2

29ft 4.5in.

13ft 0in.

34ft 5.25in.

transmitter/receivers and FuG 25 IFF (identification friend/foe) equipment. Crucially, it was discovered that the Fw 190A-2 enjoyed marginally heavier armament and a speed superior to that of the previously unassailable Spitfire V, but it was outclassed in a turning fight. If the balance had not suddenly shifted in favor of the Germans with the arrival of the A-2 in the frontline, it was at least equal. The production lines delivered 425 Fw 190A-2s between August 1941 and July 1942.

Throughout this period the pilots of JG 26 had enjoyed increasing success with the new Focke-Wulf, and with it came confidence. During March 1942, RAF Fighter Command reported the loss of 32 Spitfires and 27 pilots, while JG 26 lost just four pilots on operations. The previous month, the new *General der Jagdflieger*, Adolf Galland, had directed the Fw 190s of his former *Geschwader*, JG 26, along with the Bf 109s of JGs 1 and 2, in a complex air-cover relay operation codenamed *"Donnerkeil"*. The units were tasked with shielding three of the German Kriegsmarine's heavy ships – the battlecruisers *Scharnhorst* and *Gneisenau* and the heavy cruiser *Prinz Eugen* – as they escaped from their enforced confinement in Brest to the sanctuary of the German coast via the Straits of Dover in broad daylight. Galland succeeded and JG 26's Focke-Wulfs claimed seven enemy aircraft shot down for the loss of four of their own (of which two were Fw 190A-1s and one an A-2) and their pilots.

By March 1942 the Fw 190 had also begun to reach another *Jagdgeschwader* in the west. Following the initial, hasty, conversion of a clutch of pilots from I./JG 2 *"Richthofen"* at Le Bourget, III./JG 2, led by Knight's Cross-holder Hauptmann Hans "Assi" Hahn, took delivery of a number of A-1s at Cherbourg-Théville. The following month Hauptmann Karl-Heinz "Heino" Greisert's II. *Gruppe* at Beaumont-le-Roger and Triqueville took on A-2s, while the bulk of I./JG 2, under Hauptmann Ignaz Prestele, began to re-equip with the Fw 190A-2 at its bases at Cherbourg, St Brieuc and Morlaix.

Meanwhile, on March 4, six pilots from II./JG 1, based in Holland, travelled to Abbeville-Drucat, where they underwent a brief familiarization on II./JG 26's operationally strained Fw 190A-1s, before moving back to Rotenburg-Wümme, in northern Germany. Here, having handed in their Bf 109F-4s, they joined some 15 or more pilots in converting onto the Fw 190A-2 and A-3. By May, conversion for 4., 5. and 6./JG 1 was complete, and by the beginning of June the *Staffeln* were at Woensdrecht and Katwijk, fully equipped with the Focke-Wulf.

As early as the evening of the first day of the month, Unteroffizier Meissner of 6./JG 1 downed a Spitfire, while the following morning two Hudsons fell to the guns of Unteroffizieren Flecks and Brakebusch, both also of 6. *Staffel*. But JG 1's first big test came on June 19, when 17 Fw 190A-2s from II./JG 1 engaged a formation of 24 Spitfires over the Belgian coast. Results were mixed, with 6. *Staffel* claiming four British fighters, but sustaining two losses, including the A-2 of Unteroffizier Brakebusch. From this point on, the Fw 190s of JG 1 would be heavily committed to defending the airspace over Belgium, Holland, northwest Germany and the coast of Denmark.

During April 1942, the first Fw 190A-3 had been delivered to JG 26, with Ago and Arado having commenced production in late 1941. The A-3 was fitted with the new 1,700hp BMW 801D-2 engine, its uprated power achieved by increasing the compression ratio in the cylinders and refining the two-speed supercharger. The variant was also equipped with a pair of MG 17s and two MG 151 cannon, and it also featured a modified tail fin to accommodate an aerial antenna, as well as a redesigned cowling. Production of the A-3 continued into 1943, reaching a total of 509 machines built.

The A-2 and A-3 were delivered to *Stab*, II., III. and IV./JG 1, *Stab*, I., II., III., 10., 11. and 12./JG 2, I., III., IV. and 14.(*Jabo*)/JG 5, III. and 10./JG 11, *Stab*, I., II., III. and 10./JG 26, *Stab*, I., II., III. and 15./JG 51 and I. and II./JG 54, as well as a number of operational training *Gruppen* in the occupied territories, some reconnaissance *Staffeln* and the weapons evaluation unit *Erprobungskommando* 25.

An early production Fw 190A banks away from the camera. Even as early as the spring of 1942, the Focke-Wulf had proven itself to be both a formidable gun platform and rugged interceptor.

The A-3 was graced with the ability to adapt easily to the role of a fighter-bomber using a series of *Umbau* (modifications) – as the A-3/U1 (by means of installation of an ETC 500 bomb rack), U3 (ETC 250 fuselage rack and SC 50 underwing racks) and U7 sub-variants.

The Fw 190A-4 was developed into a fully "convertible fighter/fighter-bomber", with low-level capability provided by a Methanol-Water (MW) 50 power boost system when flying below 5,000m. Capitalizing on the A-3's adaptability, the Fw 190A-4, although carrying the same fixed armament as its predecessor, introduced an even more wide-ranging and sophisticated family of sub-variants. The A-4/U1, with only two MG 151s for armament, was fitted with two ETC 501 bomb racks for carrying a pair of SC 250 bombs, while the A-4/U3 emerged in October 1942 as a true "assault" aircraft. It was fitted with a 6mm armored ring ahead of the cowling and 5mm steel armor plates beneath the cowling and cockpit that were designed to protect the pilot, fuel tanks and engine on ground-attack missions. The A-4/U8 was a long-range fighter-bomber, fitted with a 300-liter drop tank and four SC 50 bombs on wing racks, together with full armament. Aside from the MW-50 power boost system, the A-4 also boasted an FuG 16Z VHF transceiver.

From April 1943, the Fw 190A-4 was superseded by the A-5. With the exception of a lengthened fuselage (by 15cm) and strengthened housing for the BMW 801D-2 engine, the A-5, of which 723 were built up to the summer of 1943, was essentially the same as the A-4, but Focke-Wulf made it available to the Luftwaffe with an even more inventive selection of sub-variants, reflecting the fighter's versatility. Provision was made for cannon, drop tanks, fuselage- and wing-mounted bombs and 21cm underwing air-to-air mortars for operations against formations of American bombers.

Improvements to the Fw 190, and its effectiveness as an interceptor, were seen in the steadily accumulating victory scores of several *Jagdflieger* serving in the West and the Reich in 1942–43. For example, Leutnant Josef Wurmheller of 1./JG 2 had been awarded the Oak Leaves on November 13, 1942 for shooting down seven Spitfires over the ill-fated Allied beachhead at Dieppe on August 19 of that year. This haul

took his overall tally to 60 victories. The *Staffelkapitän* of 7./JG 26, Oberleutnant Klaus Mietusch, claimed two Spitfires shot down northwest of Dieppe that same day. Two more Spitfires would fall to the guns of his Fw 190 eight days later, representing his 21st and 22nd victories. Many others would follow in Wurmheller's and Mietusch's wake by mid-1943.

In theory, Kurt Tank's robust, yet agile fighter was ideally equipped to face its new and possibly greatest challenge – the rapidly increasing numbers of heavily armed B-17 Flying Fortresses equipping the squadrons of the US Eighth Air Force on the other side of the Channel. The stakes were about to be dramatically raised.

B-17 FLYING FORTRESS

If the people of New York City needed any convincing that the senior officers of the USAAC had adhered to the principles of the Italian air power theorist Guilio Douhet, they would have only had to look to the skies over Manhattan in May 1937. There, they would have seen the sleek, silver forms of seven new four-engined Boeing Y1B-17s of the 2nd BG, which made several publicity flights during the course of the month that were designed to impress the American public and the rest of the world. USAAC air power had reached a zenith, as it had an aircraft that could protect American cities and wage war on the cities of other nations.

Work on the Y1B-17 took place between late 1935 and March 1937, but the origins of this aircraft lay in the USAAC tender of August 8, 1934, which called for a multi-engined, long-range bomber capable of delivering a one-ton bomb load. The aircraft had to be able to carry its ordnance at speeds of up to 250mph over a distance

A formation of Y1B-17s of the 2nd BG fly over New York City en route to Buenos Aires, in Argentina, on a much publicized long-distance test flight in February 1938. The aircraft had flown up from Miami, in Florida, and would return to their home field at Langley, Virginia. This was Douhet's vision upheld.

of 2,000 miles at an operating ceiling of 10,000ft. The tender-winning company could expect to be rewarded with an order for 200 such aircraft.

Among a number of manufacturers responding to the tender – which included Douglas and Martin – was Boeing of Seattle, whose engineers immediately went about enhancing the company's Model 247 all-metal commercial airliner and incorporating into the design attributes of the Model 294 bomber, including four engines (unlike the Douglas and Martin twin-engined aircraft proposals).

Spearheaded by senior company engineer Edward Curtis Wells, Boeing put everything it had into the tender, committing almost all of its available capital and labor force. A very streamlined design eventually emerged that featured a low wing with a span in excess of 100ft fitted to a cylindrical fuselage, into which could be loaded up to eight 600lb bombs. The machine was to be powered by four 750hp Pratt and Whitney R-1690-E Hornet nine-cylinder air-cooled radial engines, each driving a three-bladed propeller, and the mainwheel landing gear was to retract forward into the inner engine nacelles, with the lower edge of the wheels protruding into the airstream.

Built as the "Model 299", the aircraft was to carry a crew of eight, comprising a pilot, co-pilot, bombardier, navigator/radio operator and four gunners. Their weapons would be housed at four blister-type flexible machine gun stations in a dorsal position in the fuselage just above the wing trailing edge, in a ventral fuselage position just behind the wing trailing edge and on each side of the rear fuselage in a waist position, each of which would accommodate a 0.30-in. or 0.50-in. machine gun.

Construction of the Model 299 began on August 16, 1934, and the prototype took to the air from Seattle on July 28, 1935, with Boeing test pilot Leslie Tower at the controls. The prototype was submitted as the Model X-299 to the USAAC, but the latter objected to the designation, as it felt that it was too similar to its experimental

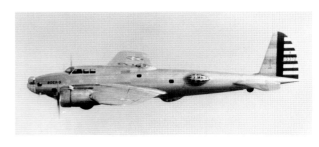

Boeing's Model 299 flew for the first time from Seattle on 28 July 1935, carrying the civilian registration X-13372, since it was a company-owned aircraft. This in-flight photograph shows clearly the blister-type machine gun stations on top of the fuselage, beneath it and one of two fuselage waist positions.

OPPOSITE
B-17G 42-39775 *FRENESI* of the 333rd BS/94th BG, based at Bury St Edmunds (Rougham) in January 1944. Piloted by 2Lt William Cely, this aircraft was finished in standard USAAF olive drab and grey, with its 94th BG black "A" marking applied within a white square on the fin. The serial number and individual aircraft letter were stencilled onto the tail fin in chrome yellow. The aircraft sustained considerable battle damage from Luftwaffe fighters while on a mission to Braunschweig on January 11, 1944 as part of the 4th Combat Wing. The aircraft was repaired once back at Rougham, and it remained with the 333rd BG until finally declared war weary and salvaged for parts in early November 1944.

military project numbers, so the aircraft officially became the B-299.

Following an impressive record-breaking flight from Seattle to the USAAC testing facility at Wright Field at Dayton, Ohio, the test program seemed to progress quite well. The Model 299 showed promise over both the Martin and Douglas designs, and exceeded all official requirements in terms of speed, climb, range and bomb load. Subsequently, the USAAC arranged to purchase 65 test machines under the designation "YB-17". Three months later, however, the aircraft crashed on take-off during testing at Wright Field, killing Tower and Ployer P. Hill, the chief of Wright Field's Flight-Testing Section. It was discovered that elevator locks had not been removed prior to flight. The accident almost rang the death knell for the Model 299 (B-299), and the USAAC cancelled any further production, with the tender award being switched to Douglas for the cheaper, but less sophisticated, B-18 Bolo.

However, in January 1936, in an apparent about-turn, the USAAC placed an order for 13 new test models under the designation "Y1B-17" – the "Y" denoted aircraft that were undergoing service testing prior to acceptance. These machines were to be assigned to the 2nd BG, under the command of Lt Col Robert C. Olds, at Langley Field, Virginia. A key change to the design saw the Y1B-17 fitted with four 930hp Wright Cyclone engines. Once again disaster was to strike when, on December 2, 1936, the very first Y1B-17 machine careered along the runway at Boeing Field following a brake failure and skidded to an ignoble stop in the midst of a Congressional investigation. Doubts grew and oblivion loomed.

Fortunately, the first Y1B-17 was delivered to the 2nd BG in March 1937, with a further 11 being phased in up to August 4 that year and the 13th aircraft going to Wright Field. This would be a critical time in the government's, the USAAC's and the public's perception of the aircraft, since the 2nd BG crews – who formed the USAAC's total heavy bomber strength – were charged with conducting a thorough assessment of the aircraft's strengths and weaknesses. "We knew if a YB crashed", recalled the 2nd BG's then 2Lt Robert F. Travis, "we could probably say goodbye to the nation's bomber program."

Fortunately, 1938 saw a series of spectacular publicity and record-breaking flights made by the 2nd BG, one of which saw Lt Col Olds set an east-to-west transcontinental record of 12 hours 50 minutes. He immediately turned around and broke the west-to-east record, averaging 245mph in 10 hours 46 minutes. Other promotional flights were made as far afield as Argentina.

Meanwhile, in January 1939 a 14th experimental aircraft (a Y1B-17A) was fitted with turbo-supercharged engines and delivered to the USAAC. Following successful trials, during which the bomber's ceiling was increased by 9,000ft and its top speed improved by 30mph at 25,000ft, an order for a further 39 such aircraft was placed under the designation B-17B (the "Y" prefix now having been dropped). Thus was born the new "Flying Fortress".

B-17G FLYING FORTRESS

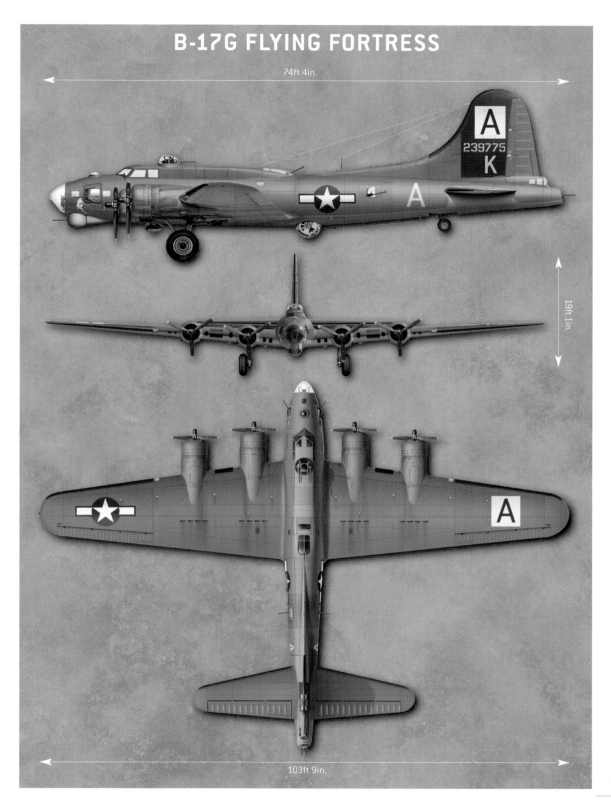

74ft 4in.

19ft 1in.

103ft 9in.

239775

The B-17 was a low-wing monoplane that combined the aerodynamic features of the Model 299 bomber project and Boeing's Model 247 airliner.

The first B-17Bs were delivered to the USAAC in 1939, equipping the 2nd and 7th BGs which conducted high-altitude precision bombing trials in California, with ostensibly encouraging results, albeit in near perfect conditions. The B-17B benefited from being powered by four 1,200hp nine-cylinder Wright R-1820-G205A engines, and in the B-17C that followed, the removal of its gun blisters gave the four gunners more workable positions with greater flexibility and field-of-fire.

The B-17D, with a wingspan just short of 104ft, featured both internal and external refinements, including improved electrical systems and further gun stations in dorsal (aft of the cockpit) and "bathtub" turrets. The latter increased the bomber's armament to an array of one 0.30-in. and six 0.50-in. machine guns. The aircraft also incorporated more "fortress"-like armor protection, while externally, engine cooling was enhanced and underwing bomb racks removed.

The B and C variants saw use in the Philippines, Hawaii and with the RAF in Britain. However, operating the aircraft as the Fortress Mk I, fitted with self-sealing fuel tanks, the RAF failed to be impressed by the Boeing design as a potential daylight bomber. One machine, which had been attacked by German fighters over Brest, in France, on July 24, 1941, effectively disintegrated on landing, while a little over two weeks earlier, Fortress Is on a raid to Wilhelmshaven were unable to defend themselves because their guns had frozen at altitude. Furthermore, they missed the target.

In September 1941 Boeing introduced the B-17E. Six feet longer than the B-17C and seven tons heavier than the original Model 299, this variant featured a substantially redesigned airframe with appreciably larger horizontal and vertical tail sections that were intended to offer the improved aerodynamic qualities necessary to make the aircraft a reliable bombing platform. It also accommodated a tail gun position – a "stinger" – for added defense. The dorsal turret was powered and the ventral turret beneath the centre fuselage section aft of the bomb-bay was remote-controlled and fitted with a periscope, resulting in a formidable total of eight 0.50-in. machine guns, with a single 0.30-in. gun mounted in a Plexiglas nose.

By the time of the Japanese attack on Pearl Harbor on December 7, 1941, the new USAAF boasted 150 B-17s on strength – the fruits of an efficient production "co-operative" of Boeing (who supplied the drawings and tooling), the Douglas Aircraft Company and the Vega Aircraft Company, a subsidiary of Lockheed. Together, they would build the B-17F.

On January 2, 1942, Maj Gen Henry "Hap" Arnold, Commanding General of the USAAF, signed the order activating the Eighth Air Force, with VIII Bomber Command being established six days later under the leadership of Brig Gen Ira C. Eaker. In August, the first B-17s flew into England via the North Atlantic ferry route, having staged via Labrador, Greenland and Prestwick in Scotland. These aircraft equipped the recently formed 97th and 301st BGs at bases in Hertfordshire and Northamptonshire (the aircraft of the 92nd BG flew direct from Newfoundland to Scotland – a distance of 2,120 miles). For the crews – despite being pitifully ill-trained on the Flying Fortress, its radio equipment and armament, and quartered a long, long way from home – it was akin to the start of a great adventure. By the end of August, a total of 119 B-17s were in England.

It was not long before the first B-17s were "blooded". In the late afternoon of August 17, a dozen Fortresses of the 97th BG, escorted by four squadrons of Spitfire Mk IXs from the RAF, bombed the marshalling yards at Sotteville, near Rouen, in occupied France, dropping 18 tons of bombs. "Going along for the ride" as an observer was Gen Eaker. Fw 190s of II./JG 26 (whose pilots wrongly identified

the bombers as British Stirlings) and JG 2 launched an attack over Ypreville. Two B-17s were lightly damaged by flak, but there were no casualties. A new dimension had opened in the air war over Europe.

The same month, the bespectacled Technical Editor of the British magazine *The Aeroplane*, Peter Masefield, visited the 97th BG at Grafton Underwood and was invited to board B-17E *Yankee Doodle*. Actually an aircraft of the 92nd BG, it had been assigned to the 97th for the Sotteville mission. Masefield recorded what he saw for his readers:

"Long, low, sleek, battle-scarred – a brown shape against the grey of the English Winter's afternoon. The interior of the Fortress is divided into seven compartments. Beginning at the rear, there is first of all the hand-operated tail gun position under the rudder. Next comes the compartment in which the retracted tail wheel is housed, and then the main rear cabin, with the two waist guns at the side, and the top of the 'ball turret' in the floor, just behind the cabin's forward bulkhead. In front of the bulkhead is the radio compartment with a 0.50-in. machine gun in the roof, and then a narrow catwalk leads through the middle of the bomb-bay to the underside of the top turret. Immediately in front of the turret is the pilot's cabin, with dual control, and seats side-by-side. Between the two pilots a little alleyway drops down and leads forward to the extreme nose, with its accommodation for navigator, bomb aimer and front gunner."

In conclusion, Masefield prophesized that "no American-manned Fortress has flown over Germany, but when the time does come, the height and speed of the Fortress formations should enable them to show up against that opposition at least as well as any other airplane of their size now flying. The question remains – are the defenses of Industrial Germany such that daylight bombing in force in good weather will result in uneconomic casualties? We may soon know the answer."

That answer would come, with startling decisiveness, in the months ahead.

With its wings and tailplane badly shot up, B-17G 42-39775 *FRENESI* of the 333rd BS/ 94th BG sits forlornly on a rain-dampened dispersal at Rougham upon its return from a mission to Braunschweig, in Germany, on January 11, 1944. *FRENESI*'s pilot, 2Lt William Cely from Houston, Texas, and co-pilot, 2Lt Jabez F. Churchill from Santa Rosa, California, can be seen standing on the port wing surveying the damage inflicted on their aircraft by German fighters. Despite the aircraft's tailplane and wings being holed, an engine knocked out and the oxygen and intercom systems rendered inoperable, *FRENESI* still made it back to Rougham – testimony to the strength and resilience of Boeing's B-17 Flying Fortress.

TECHNICAL SPECIFICATIONS

Fw 190 *STURMBÖCKE*

Fw 190A-6

Weight provided the genesis for the first variant in a series that saw Focke-Wulf redesign parts of the Fw 190, such as internal wing structure, in order to allow for greater capability and adaptation in ordnance load. Frontline units had found that the MG FF outer wing-mounted cannon did not provide sufficient firepower, and simply added disadvantageous weight on the A-5. Thus emerged the Fw 190A-6.

Originally conceived as a fighter for the Eastern Front, the A-6 was designed to accept an array of *Rustsätze* (field conversion kits) that could be added quickly to, or removed from, an airframe for mission flexibility.

Production of the Fw 190A-6 commenced in May 1943, and up to February 1944 around 1,192 machines had been built by Arado at Warnemünde, Ago at Oschersleben and Fieseler at Kassel. The aircraft was fitted with the 1,700hp BMW 801D-2 engine that was delivered by the manufacturer as a complete unit, with cowling and necessary fittings, thus allowing it to be simply hoisted into place – or changed in the field – with minimum work by means of a purpose-built harness. As such, the fully assembled unit was one of the first so-called "power eggs". It was expected that an overhaul would need to be conducted by a field unit after 100 hours of operation, with a complete depot overhaul required after two field overhauls.

The standard fuel load – and thus range – was enhanced by the installation of a centreline ETC 501 bomb rack under the fuselage between the wheel bays, to which

An Fw 190A-6 of I./JG 1 runs up its BMW 801D-2 engine outside a hangar at Dortmund airfield in early 1944. The aircraft carries a 300-liter drop tank suspended from an ETC 501 bomb rack, and its cowling is painted in the *Gruppe's* distinctive black and white horizontal bands.

could be hung a 300-liter drop tank manufactured by FRB Erla in Antwerp. When laden with fuel, the store added another 240kg of weight.

Standard armament consisted of two fuselage-mounted Rheinmetall-Borsig 7.92mm MG 17 machine guns and four electrically fired 20mm Mauser MG 151/20 cannon. The tracer ammunition of the former weapon allowed Luftwaffe pilots to sharpen their aim when using the latter.

With the Fw 190A-6/R1 (the R1 denoting the *Rüstsätze*), the outer MG 151/20s were removed and replaced with two twin-gun underwing WB151/20 cannon pods located outboard of the undercarriage legs. The first 60 such aircraft were delivered by LZA Küpper on 20 November 1943. There were brief trials that saw the WB151/20s replaced by a 30mm MK 108 cannon to become the A-6/R2. This weapon fit was trialed by prototype Fw 190 V51 (formerly an A-6), which had been fitted with pods for the MK 108 by Fieseler.

The MK 108 of late 1943 was a blowback-operated, rear-seared, belt-fed cannon that used electric ignition, the latter being charged and triggered by compressed air. The prime benefit of this weapon, which would be widely used to devastating effect by the Luftwaffe for close-range anti-bomber work over northwest and southern Europe, lay in its simplicity and economic process of manufacture. Indeed, the majority of its components consisted of pressed sheet metal stampings.

Fieseler was also chosen to work on the A-6/R6, which was equipped with a WGr. 21cm mortar braced to each wing that was intended for operations against formations of four-engined bombers. The company began producing this variant straight from the factory as a retro-fit, using the *Änderungs Anweisung* (Conversion Pack) *No. 123* in November 1943.

Another sub-variant, the A-6/R4, featured a GM1 nitrous oxide injection power boost system for the BMW 801 engine.

In the cockpit area, the sliding canopy benefited from the protection of 30mm thick armored glass, which was also used in the windshield panel. However, of particular interest to this study is that in the A-6, the cockpit sides were reinforced by 5mm armor plate, which when combined with the assigned armament configuration transformed the aircraft into the Fw 190A-6/R7.

This variant also carried an FuG 16 ZE VHF transceiver, with a *Peilrahmen* PR 16 loop antenna located under the rear fuselage for radio navigation.

With the incorporation of such *Rüstsatze*, the A-6 was effectively the first Fw 190 type to be able to hold its own against the massed defensive firepower of USAAF B-17 formations, and to be sufficiently armed to wreak considerable destruction upon them.

The Fw 190A-6 was delivered to several units that subsequently saw action against the B-17 in the mid-war period, namely *Stab*, I. and II./JG 1, *Stab*, I. and III./JG 2, IV./JG 3, *Stab*, I., III. and 10./JG 11, *Stab*, I., II. and 10./JG 26, *Stab* and II./JG 300, *Stab* JG 301, II. and III./JG 302, *Sturmstaffel* 1 and *E.Kdo* 25.

Fw 190A-7

The short-run, interim, Fw 190A-7 evolved in November 1943, but it did not appear until January 1944 (Focke-Wulf having completed its tooling up by December 1943). It differed from the A-5 in having the fuselage-mounted 7.92mm MG 17 armament replaced by 13mm MG 131 machine guns, which in turn necessitated the working in of extended longitudinal bulges with access panels to house the new, larger weapons. The MG 131s supplemented the existing four MG 151/20E wing-mounted cannon, and the aircraft could be augmented by the fitting of R1, R2 and R6 *Rüstsätze*. The R2 conversion is believed to have accounted for half the production run of just 80 or so aircraft built by Focke-Wulf at Cottbus, Ago and Fieseler, and it was intended as a *"schwerer Jäger"*, or "heavy fighter", for deployment against Allied heavy bombers. Such examples were delivered to JGs 1, 2, 11 and 26 from early March 1944.

Externally, an ETC 501 centreline rack was fitted for the carriage of a 300-liter drop tank to extend range, and provisions were made on some examples for a

Hauptmann Alfred Grislawski, *Staffelkapitän* of 1./JG 1, stands on the wing root of his Fw 190A-7 Wk-Nr 430965 "White 9" at Dortmund in January 1944. The aircraft was adapted to fly night operations, and thus had flash suppressors fitted over the engine-mounted 13mm machine guns. It also had an armored windscreen, and carried the emblem of JG 1, the red defense of the Reich band of the *Geschwader* and what is believed to be a yellow lower engine cowling panel. This aircraft was lost on February 22, 1944 in combat with USAAF heavy bombers while being flown by Gefreiter Alfred Martini of 2./JG 1.

completely revised tail wheel arrangement. In the cockpit, the Revi C/12D gunsight was replaced by the new *Reflexvisier* Revi 16B sight, and a simplified radio system with no screening was fitted.

A few *Staffeln*, including some within JG 2, flew the Fw 190A-7/R2/R6, which carried both 30mm MK 108 cannon as well as underwing Werfergranate WGr. 21cm mortars, as a *Pulk Zerstörer* – a "bomber formation destroyer". Some machines built by Fieseler at Kassel incorporated the MK 108 in their outer wings.

Fw 190A-7s were delivered to *Stab*, I. and II./JG 1, *Stab*, I. and II./JG 2, IV./JG 3, I., II. and III./JG 11, *Stab*, I. and II./JG 26, *Stab* and II./JG 300, *Stab*/JG 301, *Sturmstaffel* 1, *E.Kdo* 25 and *Jagdgruppe* 10. All of these units opposed the USAAF's daylight bombing raids.

Fw 190A-8

The Fw 190A-8 was by far the most numerous and most potent Fw 190 heavy fighter to be built, with 1,334 produced between Focke-Wulf at Cottbus and Aslau, Ago at Oschersleben, Fieseler at Kassel, Weserflug at Tempelhof and Norddeutsche Dornier at Wismar. These numbers in turn meant that it was the Luftwaffe's main close-range interceptor for operations against USAAF heavy bombers throughout 1944–45.

Powered by the 1,700hp BMW 801D-2 14-cylinder radial air-cooled engine, it could attain a top speed of 647km/h at 5,500m, reaching 656km/h with GM 1 nitrous oxygen boost. Fuel was held in two self-sealing tanks (of 232 and 292 liters, respectively) beneath the cockpit, but another 115 liters could be carried in the area normally assigned to the GM 1 fuel tank or MW-50 methanol-water boost. Range was 1,035km at 7,000m, extending to 1,470km when carrying a 300-liter drop tank.

Armament was formidable. Although the standard configuration was based on the A-7, the A-8 could be converted into an R1 with four MG 151s under the wings, but due to an ensuing reduction in performance, series production of this pack was

Leutnant Werner Gerth of 11.(*Sturm*)/JG 3 flew this Fw 190A-8/R2 "Black 13", which was fitted with additional side armor, during the summer of 1944. Born in May 1923 in Pforzheim, Gerth served with 7./JG 53 in the summer of 1943, before volunteering for *Sturmstaffel* 1 in January 1944. Here, he became one of the unit's most successful pilots. Eventually appointed *Staffelkapitän* of 11./JG 3 on April 20, 1944, Gerth was awarded the Knight's Cross in October 1944 after 27 victories. He was killed in action on November 2, 1944 while *Staffelkapitän* of 14./JG 3. Having rammed an enemy bomber, Gerth attempted to bail out of his crippled fighter, but his parachute failed to open. By the time of his death he had claimed a total of 27 victories, of which at least 16 are believed to have been B-17s.

discontinued on April 8, 1944. The A-8/R2 had the outer MG 151s replaced by 30mm MK 108 cannon mounted within the wings, as this was better suited to close-range destructive work. The A-8/R3 carried a gas-operated, air-cooled Rheinmetall 30mm MK 103 cannon in a pod under each wing, having a rate of fire of 450rpm. Like the MK 108, the MK 103 had parts stamped out of sheet metal.

The A-8/R7 had 5mm armor plating protecting the MK 108s and cockpit and had 30mm *Panzerglas* ("armored glass") side panels fitted in the canopy. The A-8/R8 was a *Sturmflugzeug* ("assault aircraft") that included armored glass and a built-in MK 108 in the wing outboard position. Commonplace also on the A-8 were twin under-wing 21cm mortars, the fittings for which were built in as standard.

Radio equipment comprised the FuG 16 ZY VHF transceiver with a Morane whip aerial array and, from June 1944, a 16mm BSK (*Ballistische Schußmeßkammer*) 16 camera was installed in the leading edge of the port wing between the cannon.

Fw 190A-8/R2 WING GUNS

The Fw 190A-7, A-8 and A-9 variants fielded a pair of fuselage-mounted Rheinmetall-Borsig 13mm MG 131 machine guns, supplemented by four Mauser 20mm MG 151/20E wing-mounted cannon in the wing roots and outer wing sections. The A-8/R2 had its outer MG 151s replaced by the 30mm MK 108 cannon in the wings, and these proved to be far better suited to close-range operations against four-engined bombers. The A-8/R3 carried a Rheinmetall 30mm MK 103 cannon in a pod under each wing, firing at a rate of 450 rounds per minute.

The Fw 190A-8 was flown operationally by *Stab*, I. and II./JG 1, *Stab*, I. and III./JG 2, *Stab* and IV./JG 3, *Stab* and II./JG 4, *Stab*, I. and II./JG 6, *Stab*, I., III. and 10./JG 11, *Stab*, I. and II./JG 26, *Stab* and II./JG 300, *Stab*, I., II. and III./JG 301, I./JG 302, *Sturmstaffel* 1, *E.Kdo* 25 and *Jagdgruppe* 10.

B-17 FLYING FORTRESS

B-17E

The USAAF's Eighth Air Force launched its bomber war against Nazi Germany with the Boeing B-17E. The first examples of this magnificent and quite majestic four-engined

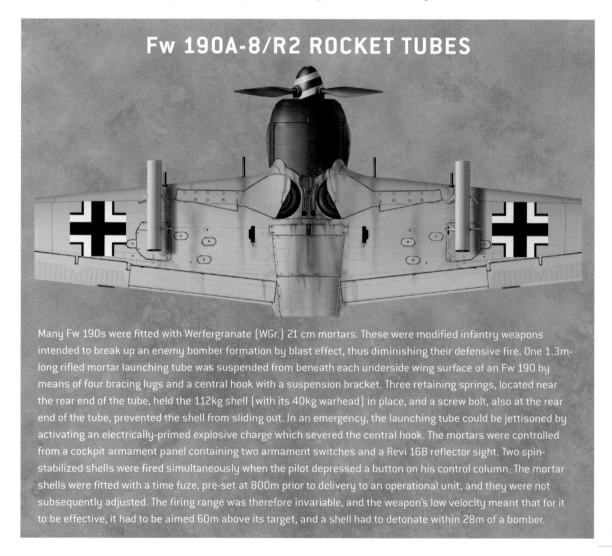

Fw 190A-8/R2 ROCKET TUBES

Many Fw 190s were fitted with Werfergranate (WGr.) 21 cm mortars. These were modified infantry weapons intended to break up an enemy bomber formation by blast effect, thus diminishing their defensive fire. One 1.3m-long rifled mortar launching tube was suspended from beneath each underside wing surface of an Fw 190 by means of four bracing lugs and a central hook with a suspension bracket. Three retaining springs, located near the rear end of the tube, held the 112kg shell (with its 40kg warhead) in place, and a screw bolt, also at the rear end of the tube, prevented the shell from sliding out. In an emergency, the launching tube could be jettisoned by activating an electrically-primed explosive charge which severed the central hook. The mortars were controlled from a cockpit armament panel containing two armament switches and a Revi 16B reflector sight. Two spin-stabilized shells were fired simultaneously when the pilot depressed a button on his control column. The mortar shells were fitted with a time fuze, pre-set at 800m prior to delivery to an operational unit, and they were not subsequently adjusted. The firing range was therefore invariable, and the weapon's low velocity meant that for it to be effective, it had to be aimed 60m above its target, and a shell had to detonate within 28m of a bomber.

bomber rolled off the production line in September 1941 and arrived in England in July 1942. Seven tons heavier and 40 percent faster than Boeing's original Model 299, it represented an extensive redesign and improvement over the earlier C and D variants, with a major aerodynamic reworking of the tail section and rear fuselage areas in order to improve stability for bombing. Most evident was the distinctive, low, sweeping fillet that pulled back from halfway along the fuselage as part of an extended tail assembly.

The fuselage of the B-17 was formed from an all-metal, semi-monocoque structure constructed of Alclad fastened with alloy rivets, and within which was built a number of bulkheads separating four sections. These comprised the forward section housing the bombardier-navigator's and pilots' compartments, the centre section containing the bomb-bay, the rear fuselage section and the tail section. Internally, there was a maximum cross-section height of 103 inches. and a maximum width of 90 inches.

The B-17E had a semi-monocoque wing with a span of 103ft 9in. (1,486ft wing area), and the aircraft was 73ft 10in. in length. Power was provided by four up-rated 1,200hp Wright Cyclone R-1820-65s, which increased maximum speed to 323mph at 25,000ft – an improvement over the B-17C/D. The wings held three fuel tanks in their inboard sections and nine outboard, with a total capacity of 2,780 US gallons. Normal range was 2,000 miles. Empty, the aircraft weighed 32,250lbs.

The extreme rear fuselage had also been extended and enlarged to accommodate a tail gun turret, mounting twin 0.50-in. Browning M-2 machine guns for anticipated defense against fighter attack from the rear. These were hand-operated by a gunner in a sit-kneel position. Additionally, a dorsal 360 degree-turn power-operated turret built by Sperry was installed into the upper fuselage immediately aft of the cockpit, while a remotely controlled Bendix ventral turret, fitted with a periscope sight to be used by a gunner in a prone position, was installed in the underside of the central fuselage aft of the bomb-bay. Both these turrets also fielded twin Brownings, turning the B-17E into a proper "Flying Fortress", armed with eight 0.50-in. guns in total and a single 0.30-in. nose-mounted weapon in a framed nose cone.

There were two major disadvantages that stemmed from this design, however. Firstly, the Bendix turret proved unsatisfactory, and secondly, the resultant drag from the turrets and the enlarged tail assembly reduced top speed by some 6 mph.

Although the B-17E was a most welcome addition to US air power, by January 1942 the Boeing plant at Seattle, which had received an order for 512 E-models in the summer of 1940, was producing only around two to three machines per day. And while, on paper, the USAAF boasted 14 heavy bomb groups, only three were fully equipped with B-17s. It seems that agreements signed with Douglas and Lockheed-Vega did little to overcome the slow rate of production.

The B-17E first saw operational service with the USAAF against the Japanese in the Philippines shortly after Pearl Harbor, and also in India, from where missions were flown against the enemy advance through Burma. In early 1942, B-17s flew from northern Australia and then over the Southwest Pacific, where they met with considerable success in anti-shipping attacks.

However, there were tactical lessons learned. Japanese fighter pilots had quickly identified that the head-on attack against the B-17E exploited its weakest point of defense, while Fortress crews soon came to learn that the ventral turret was actually quite impractical. Thus, the nose armament was beefed up by removing the 0.30-in. gun and replacing it with one or two 0.50-in. guns, while crews elected to remove the ventral turret to save on weight. But none of these early operations could be termed "strategic bombing" of the kind that would be needed in the coming European war.

The B-17 had been conceived essentially as a medium bomber whose range and endurance had been optimized in a trade-off against the aircraft's bombload, which stood at just 4,000lbs – the British Avro Lancaster of comparable size could carry a payload of 14,000lbs. The bomb-bay doors of the B-17 were a modest 11ft long, compared to those of the Lancaster which measured 33ft.

Forty-nine B-17Es were eventually ferried to England for the 97th BG. Before leaving the US, the aircraft had their side gun windows enlarged and, on arrival on the other side of the Atlantic, further modifications were carried out that included improvements to the aircraft's radio. Some shortcomings were also noted in oxygen, bomb rack, lighting, fire extinguisher and life raft equipment.

The B-17E did not enjoy a long period of service, being "moved aside" to make way for the F-model, the improved performance of which made joint operations between the two types problematic. Apart from performing a small number of combat missions, the type was relegated to an operational training role with the Combat Crew Replacement Center (CCRC) at Bovingdon in early 1943. By the summer of that year, B-17Es were being used for training, liaison, ambulance, transport or target-towing duties. Nevertheless, the E-model formed an admirable platform for the development of the renowned variants that would follow it.

A USAAF gunner demonstrates the method of exit from the claustrophobic confines of the Sperry ball turret beneath a B-17. The gunner in this station would, out of necessity, be of smaller build. The turret was suspended by a tubular member anchored to a spine box between two reinforced formers. The gunner was unable to enter the turret from the interior of the aircraft when it was on the ground since there was insufficient ground clearance for the Browning machine gun barrels when vertical – the only position in which the turret door would have been accessible from inside the fuselage. Once inside the turret, the gunner would be accommodated like an embryo, with his knees and feet level with his head. Ammunition was also stored in the turret.

B-17F

The USAAF's first truly combat-ready version of the Fortress, refined following experience in the Pacific and from early operations conducted over England with the RAF (which had used both the D- and E-nodels as the Fortress I and II, respectively) and the Eighth Air Force, the B-17F actually differed very little from its immediate predecessor. In fact, the F-model's main distinguishing external feature was its new frameless nose cone. Internally, however, some 400 minor changes had been undertaken! These included re-engineering the leading edge contours of the cowlings of the four

B-17G ARMAMENT FIELDS-OF-FIRE

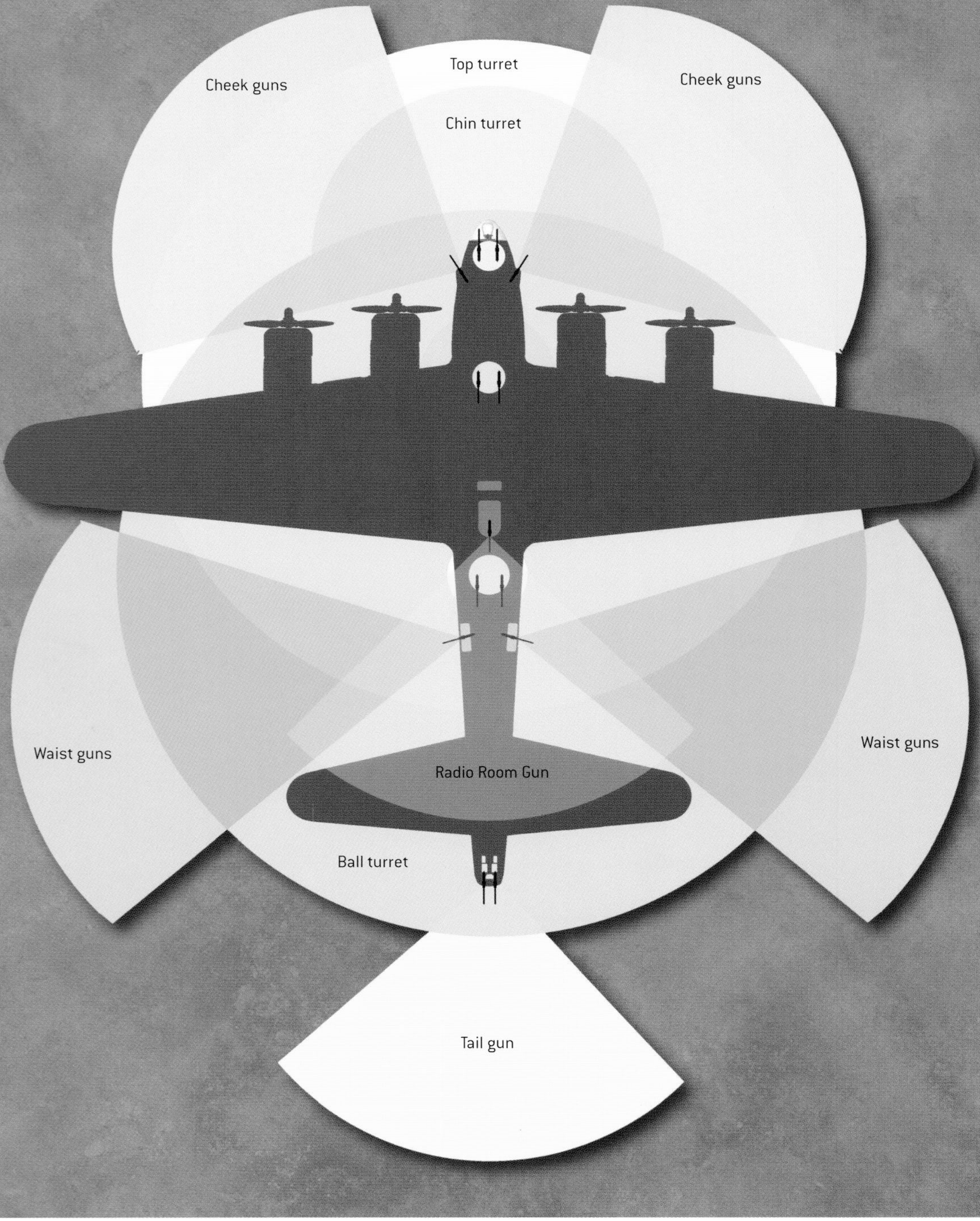

Cheek guns

Top turret

Chin turret

Cheek guns

Waist guns

Radio Room Gun

Waist guns

Ball turret

Tail gun

1,200 hp Wright R-120-97 radial engines to avoid the new Hamilton Standard "paddle blade" propellers striking them when feathered, as well as improvements to the oxygen system (which suffered from inadequate supply and freezing), landing gear and brakes. Enhancements were also made to the bomb racks and ball turret (the least favored position in the aircraft, where excess ice and oil played havoc with the guns), and an automatic pilot/bombsight link was installed.

The first F-models were delivered by Boeing Seattle in late May 1942, with Douglas at Long Beach and Lockheed-Vega following during the summer. By August 1943, all three plants accounted for an average output of 400 aircraft per month.

In terms of armament, the lessons learned in the Pacific resulted in the fitting of a 0.50-in. Browning M-2 in each of two newly created Plexiglas observation windows either side of the nose, to be used by either the bombardier or the navigator. These additions meant that the B-17F (by this stage the most heavily armed bomber in service) carried 12 or 13 machine guns. However, not all machines benefited from this modification, and many soldiered on into early 1943 with the nose adapted to accommodate a 0.50-in. gun with a mounting able to absorb the increased recoil.

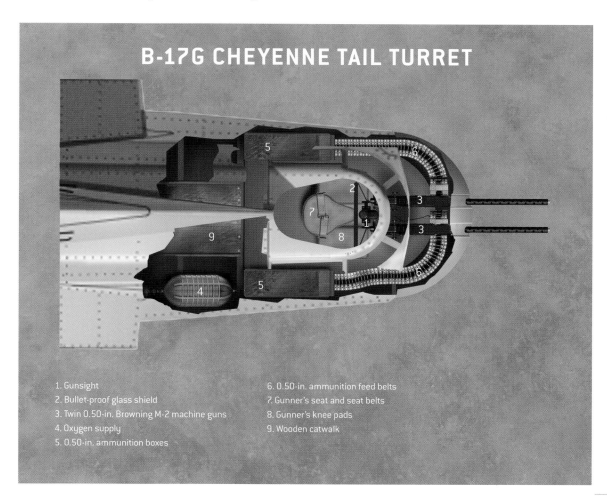

B-17G CHEYENNE TAIL TURRET

1. Gunsight
2. Bullet-proof glass shield
3. Twin 0.50-in. Browning M-2 machine guns
4. Oxygen supply
5. 0.50-in. ammunition boxes
6. 0.50-in. ammunition feed belts
7. Gunner's seat and seat belts
8. Gunner's knee pads
9. Wooden catwalk

The B-17G featured a frameless Plexiglas nose cone, below which was fitted a twin-gun Bendix "chin" turret that was positioned immediately beneath the bombardier's seat on a pivot housing for lateral rotation. The remote control for operating the turret and its 0.50-in. Browning M-2 was mounted on a tubular bracket, which could be clipped away to starboard and swung quickly into a central position for operation. The twin hand grips — known as "dead man's handles" — had small inserts which, when depressed, made an electrical contact in the turret operation circuit. The handles' movement controlled the relative movement of both turret and guns, as well as the reflector sight in the upper section of the nose cone.

RIGHT
A sting in the tail. The Cheyenne tail turret provided greater all-round vision and field-of-fire for the tail gunner in a B-17G, as well as offering an improved form of defense from German fighter attack. The latter, when executed *en masse* by Luftwaffe *Sturmgruppen*, often came from the bomber's rear.

B-17G

The B-17G was the last production model of the B-17 series, with first examples being delivered to the USAAF from September 1943. These were in turn deployed on operations conducted by the Eighth Air Force the following month, early aircraft taking part in the second Schweinfurt raid alongside B-17Fs. Effectively an organic development of the F-model, the G is perhaps best identified by its Bendix "chin" turret, which was fitted with twin 0.50-in. Browning M-2s, and intended as an antidote to Luftwaffe head-on fighter attacks.

First introduced on some of the last B-17Fs, the chin turret was designed to be operated under remote control by the bombardier, but its installation forced the removal of the direction-finding loop originally housed in a streamlined fairing. This equipment was re-installed just forward of the bomb-bay and a little to the left of the fuselage centreline.

The Sperry upper turret was replaced by a Bendix type that offered improved visibility and control. The earlier design of the tail turret, which featured a tunnel opening at the very end of the fuselage, was changed for a new Cheyenne turret — named after the town in Wyoming where it had been designed at the United Air Lines Modification Center — which provided larger windows, giving better visibility, a greater field-of-fire and a reflector sight for the tail gunner. This was a great improvement over the former turret's 30-degree traverse and primitive ring and bead sight positioned outside and beyond the much smaller gunner's window. The guns were moved nearer the gunner and the mounting protected by a semi-circular cover.

In its usual form, the B-17G brandished no fewer than 13 0.50-in. Browning M-2 machine guns, two each in the chin, upper, ball and tail turrets, with further such weapons in the nose cheek positions and waist windows.

A *Flight* magazine journalist who inspected the B-17G summarized, "The Flying Fortress is now, after its nine years of development, a very good military aircraft, well liked by its crews, sturdy of build and eminently capable of both taking and handing out great punishment."

THE STRATEGIC SITUATION

The strategic air offensive against Germany is credited with bringing about the Third Reich's inability to continue the war. For nearly three years, by day and night, the Allies pulverized Germany's cities and factories, paralyzed its transport system, terrorized and killed its civilians and eventually smashed its armies as they defended their ever-shrinking territory. The Luftwaffe, charged with defending the home skies, found it difficult to resist. A bitter battle of attrition tested both its material and human resources to their limits.

Since the opening of its operations in August 1942 to the end of that year, the Eighth Air Force's VIII Bomber Command (VIII BC), commanded by Brig Gen Ira C Eaker, had been "blooded" in 30 daylight missions flown from its airfields across eastern England to maritime, industrial, airfield and railway targets in France and the Low Countries. On most occasions the bombers enjoyed RAF fighter escort. VIII BC had been progressively reinforced and expanded throughout the second half of 1942 to the point where it numbered six bomb groups – four equipped with B-17Fs and two with B-24Ds. On January 20, 1943, Eaker handed Prime Minister Winston Churchill a memorandum in which were outlined his reasons for the pursuance of such daylight attacks. "By bombing the devils around the clock", Eaker wrote, "we can prevent the German defenses from getting any rest."

This was just what Churchill wanted to read, and the very next day, during the Allied Leaders' conference in Casablanca, the air commanders were told, "Given a force of 300 heavy bombers flown by trained crews, Gen Eaker believed he could attack any target in Germany by day with less than four per cent loss. Smaller numbers would naturally suffer more severely. Despite all problems and currently

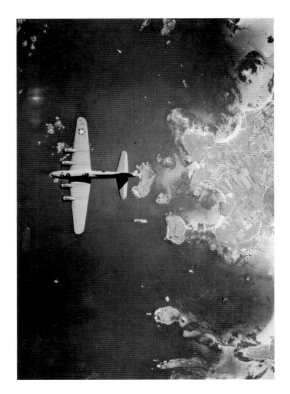

B-17F 42-5243 *FDR's Potato Peeler Kids* of the the 359th BS/303rd BG, 1st BW, leaves the French coast, having bombed U-boat pens at Brest on February 27, 1943.

effective limitations, he stoutly maintained that 'daylight bombing of Germany with airplanes of the B-17 and B-24 types is feasible, practicable and economical'."

A month later, on April 17, the Eighth Air Force unveiled its new, more concentrated type of defensive flight formation for the war against Germany. In the first such deployment, two "combat wings" comprising 107 B-17s in six "boxes" – the largest force thus far assembled – were despatched on this date to bomb the Focke-Wulf plant at Bremen. On this occasion, the wings ran into tough defense. Just after the "heavies" had commenced their bomb run, the Fw 190s of I. and II./JG 1 closed in at speed and mauled the B-17s for an hour. In determined, well-coordinated head-on attacks, JG 1 accounted for 15 Flying Fortresses destroyed, including an entire squadron – the heaviest losses sustained to date in a single mission. For their part, the American gunners excessively claimed 63 fighters shot down and another 15 "probables". Just one German aircraft was actually lost in combat.

Despite these setbacks, Eaker acknowledged that his bombers had proven their ability to successfully penetrate the German defenses, but that continued success depended on the quick expansion of his command. He asked for a further 944 B-17s by July, 1,192 by October, 1,746 by January 1944 and 2,702 by April. In the short term, however, May 13, 1943 saw the arrival of six new bomb groups to strengthen VIII BC. Eaker recorded that it was "a great day".

On May 4, P-47 Thunderbolts flew as escorts for the first time, accompanying 65 B-17s to bomb Antwerp. However, the problem of providing an escort all the way to German targets would remain until a workable drop tank design had been found. In the meantime, the tactical radius of the P-47 (250 miles) took it into the Low Countries and as far as the Rhine, but not beyond. From thereon, the Fortresses would be on their own, flying into the teeth of the increasingly hardening German defenses.

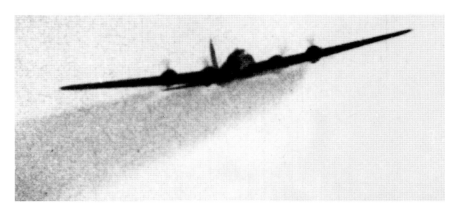

A B-17F trails smoke following a Luftwaffe fighter attack in 1943 .

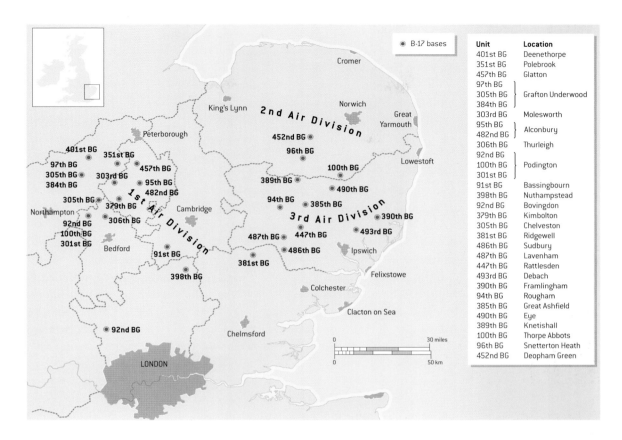

Unit	Location
401st BG	Deenethorpe
351st BG	Polebrook
457th BG	Glatton
97th BG	
305th BG	Grafton Underwood
384th BG	
303rd BG	Molesworth
95th BG	
482nd BG	Alconbury
306th BG	Thurleigh
92nd BG	
100th BG	Podington
301st BG	
91st BG	Bassingbourn
398th BG	Nuthampstead
92nd BG	Bovingdon
379th BG	Kimbolton
305th BG	Chelveston
381st BG	Ridgewell
486th BG	Sudbury
487th BG	Lavenham
447th BG	Rattlesden
493rd BG	Debach
390th BG	Framlingham
94th BG	Rougham
385th BG	Great Ashfield
490th BG	Eye
389th BG	Knetishall
100th BG	Thorpe Abbots
96th BG	Snetterton Heath
452nd BG	Deopham Green

As for the Combined Bomber Offensive proposed at Casablanca, there was little sign of it achieving its objective. Both commanders and crews began to realize that the destruction of Germany was going to be a long haul.

A redistribution of its fighter strength in the spring and summer of 1943 meant that the Luftwaffe was able to pursue a policy of "Defense in Depth". This meant that by expanding its defensive zones along the coast of northwest Europe, and by simultaneously holding the bulk of its fighter strength back in the Reich, German fighters would be beyond the range of US fighters, and therefore able to concentrate their efforts exclusively on the bombers. Furthermore, fighter production had been increasing steadily throughout the first seven months of 1943.

By July 1, there were approximately 800 single-engined fighters available for the daylight defense of the Reich and the West, but they were being steadily depleted in a growing battle of attrition against the Allied air forces at a rate that was difficult to sustain. In July 1943, German fighter losses (all fronts) stood at 31.2 percent, while the loss in single-engined fighter pilots (all fronts and all causes) in July stood at 330, or 16 percent – an increase of 84 pilots on the previous month. Even harder to bear was the accumulating loss of experienced unit commanders.

The same month, in a turning point for USAAF fighter operations, P-47s of the 4th FG appeared for the first time in German skies fitted with auxiliary fuel tanks that greatly extended their range.

The US Eighth Air Force's infrastructure of nearly 30 B-17 bases sprawled across much of the English northern Home Counties and East Anglia, with the three air divisions managing tactical and logistical control. More than 30 B-17 groups equipped the Eighth, in addition to B-24, fighter and support squadrons and groups.

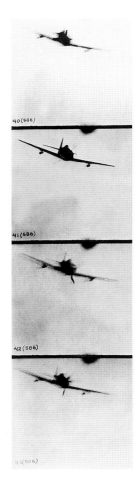

A sequence of stills taken from a USAAF bomber showing an Fw 190 coming in at close range to launch an attack during the raid to Kassel and Oschersleben on July 28, 1943. Clearly visible are the underwing 21 cm air-to-air mortars, which have probably already been fired, allowing the pilot to make his attack with guns.

On August 17, 1943 – the anniversary of its first heavy raid on northern Europe, VIII BC launched its notorious attack against the ball-bearing center of Schweinfurt. Sixty B-17s were shot down and 168 damaged. The destruction inflicted upon the factories did not compensate for the loss of more than 600 Allied airmen, especially when German production was interrupted for only a few weeks.

The Luftwaffe fighter force was able to celebrate a cautious victory, despite the fact that the losses for all participating *Geschwader* amounted to 17 killed and 14 wounded, with 42 aircraft lost. The losses incurred that day included Major Wilhelm-Ferdinand "Wutz" Galland, *Kommandeur* of II./JG 26, a most respected formation leader with 55 kills to his credit (including eight "heavies") and brother to Adolf Galland.

Schweinfurt had provided the Luftwaffe with vital tactical lessons, and on September 3 Adolf Galland issued revised directives to every fighter *Staffel* engaged in the defense of the Reich. Paramount in these new directives was the order for units to engage only *one* enemy wave of attack "continuously" with "the mass of all fighter units".

The "heavies" returned to Germany on 6 September, when VIII BC mounted its largest mission to date by sending 338 B-17s to bomb aircraft component factories in Stuttgart. Thick cloud hampered the operation from the start and many Fortresses failed to bomb, 233 of them opting for targets of opportunity on their return leg. One of the German units to engage the bombers was Hauptmann Walther Dahl's III./JG 3 with 25 Bf 109G-6s. As the Messerschmitts – some of them carrying mortars – turned south towards Stuttgart, the bombers were sighted and the fighters went in to attack. Within 30 minutes, the *Gruppe* had claimed four B-17s shot down and eight cut out of formation, with Dahl claiming one of each. As a result of disorganization and separation, 45 B-17s were lost in total, amounting to 16 percent of the total force in one of the costliest missions so far. More than 300 crew were posted missing.

In October 1943, the daylight battle over the Reich reached its zenith, forcing the Americans to accept that unescorted, deep penetration formations could not adequately protect themselves. Yet though the losses incurred during such missions reached unacceptable levels, they nevertheless forced the Luftwaffe into the air to fight, and in doing so inflicted attrition on a scale from which the Germans would find it difficult to recover.

On October 14, 229 B-17s went to Schweinfurt again – a destination that had proved so costly in August. Because of fog, just two fighter groups were able to undertake escort for the bombers. Later, as the weather cleared, the Luftwaffe committed all of its daylight fighter units, drawn from five fighter divisions – a total of 567 machines, as well as twin-engined *Zerstörer* and some fighter training school aircraft and nightfighters. By the time the 1st BD entered the target area, it had lost 36 bombers, with one group alone losing just under half its strength. By the time the mission was over, the division's losses had increased to 45 machines. One combat wing of 37 aircraft had lost 21 aircraft. German losses were 31 aircraft destroyed, 12 written off and 34 damaged – between 3.4 and 4 percent of available fighter strength in the West. One senior German air commander recorded "the units of the German *Reichsverteidigung* achieved a great defensive success on October 14, 1943".

B-17s of the Eighth Air Force's 94th BG head for home after bombing the Focke-Wulf plant at Marienburg on October 9, 1943. For the first time, the B-17s dropped 100lb jellied gasoline incendiary bombs on this mission. The Marienburg facility was responsible for nearly 50 percent of Fw 190 output at the time. The B-17s, flying at 11,000–13,000ft, dropped 60 percent of their bombs within 1,000ft of their intended point of impact, while 83 percent fell within 2,000ft. Gen Ira Eaker described the results as "a classic example of precision bombing".

For the Americans, the second Schweinfurt raid had cost VIII BC another 59 B-17s and nearly 600 aircrew. Seventeen more bombers were seriously damaged and a further 121 were damaged but repairable. It was a body blow. Despite the catastrophe, a buoyant Eaker wrote that the Luftwaffe's response was "pretty much the last final struggles of a monster in his death throes". Gen Arnold was unconvinced, however, and replied, "The cornered wolf fights hardest."

Certainly, the losses from Schweinfurt forced a halt in the progressive American strategy of hitting deep penetration targets until such time that greater numbers of long-range escort fighters were available and missions were kept within range of them. Although it could not be said by any means the Luftwaffe was *winning* the battle for air superiority over Europe, it was nevertheless preventing the USAAF from doing so. Equally, however, on the German side, with 67 percent of production at Schweinfurt knocked out, the ball-bearing industry was forced to disperse its manufacturing capacity, which in turn presented logistics problems.

On November 8, 1943, Galland advised his units that Göring wanted to form a *Sturmstaffel*, which would press home attacks to the very heart of an Allied formation without regard to losses. Volunteers were called for. On January 1, 1944, Arnold sent a simple message to his commanders to welcome the New Year: "Destroy the enemy air force wherever you find them – in the air, on the ground, and in the factories."

January saw the Luftwaffe suffer a staggering 30.3 percent loss of its single-engined fighters and 16.9 percent of fighter pilots. Furthermore, the beginning of the year showed a percentage decrease in the Luftwaffe's Order of Battle for Bf 109 and Fw 190 interceptors from 31 percent in 1943 to 27 percent at the beginning of 1944.

New threats were developing for the Germans, however. From the south, the USAAF's Fifteenth Air Force began to attack targets in Austria and southern Germany, and then in February, the Eighth Air Force launched Operation *Argument*, or "Big

Under attack! A photograph taken from a B-17 captures the moment an Fw 190 makes a frontal attack through an American bomber formation over Bremen in November 1943.

Incredulity spreads across the faces of Eighth Air Force bomber crews at the briefing room at Polebrook air base in England in the early hours of March 6, 1944. Their target for the day was Berlin – a new milestone in the daylight bomber offensive.

Week" – a concerted bombing campaign against the fighter production plants. The offensive was intended to do two things – destroy German aircraft on the ground (and the means of replacing them) and force the Luftwaffe into the air to defend the Reich against the attacks. In all, 16 combat wings of heavy bombers totaling 1,000 aircraft were committed to the operation, together with fighter protection from all available groups in both the Eighth and Ninth Air Forces. It was to be the largest force ever assembled in the history of American strategic air power.

Between them, the German I. and II. *Jagdkorps* could muster approximately 750 serviceable aircraft. Yet, in the main, the flying and combat skills of most of the ill-trained pilots comprising the component *Geschwader* were questionable.

Major Sturm bases 1944

Line of defense. The Luftwaffe deployed its *Sturmgruppen* in a wall of bases stretching across central Germany, close to the main industrial targets and in the direct path of bomber incursions approaching from England. From these bases, they would have time to assemble into *Gefechtsverband* (air battle group) strength in order to engage the bombers *en masse*.

In March, the Americans felt sufficiently confident to concentrate their efforts on Berlin – the "hub" of Germany's war effort. The first strike was mounted on March 4, when a force of 500 B-17s and B-24s, escorted by 770 fighters, headed for the capital. The concept was not solely to bomb industrial targets, nor even to dent civilian morale, but rather to coax the Jagdwaffe into the air in order to inflict further unsustainable losses. The trump card was the P-51B Mustang. Equipped with twin 108-gallon wing tanks, this new fighter was now able to escort the bombers as far as the German capital.

In a second raid on Berlin on March 6, the Luftwaffe suffered 87 fighters lost or damaged, 36 pilots killed and 27 wounded. Among those to die were the *Ritterkreuzträger* Oberleutnant Gerhard Loos of III./JG 54, who had 92 victories to his credit, and Leutnant Hugo Frey, *Staffelkapitän* of 7./JG 11. He had claimed four bombers shot down earlier in the day, prior to being killed over Holland. Frey's overall tally of 32 victories included 26 four-engined bombers.

On the American side, 53 B-17s failed to return, while 293 were damaged and five written off. Seventeen crew were killed, 31 wounded and 686 listed as missing. It was the highest loss rate suffered by VIII BC to date. Both sides withdrew to lick their wounds and assess their losses. Both sides questioned whether such targets were worth the cost. But of even greater psychological impact on the Germans was the fact that Berlin could

Nemesis for the Jagdwaffe: in one its early appearances, a P-51B Mustang keeps watch on a "box" of B-17s during a long-range mission to a German target.

B-17s of the 303rd BG brave a barrage of flak on their way to Berlin on March 6, 1944. The Flying Fortresses would also encounter many Luftwaffe fighters, and suffer heavy losses – 53 B-17s failed to return from this mission, while 293 were damaged and five written off as result of the raid.

no longer be considered immune from attack. From this point, the pressure on the pilots of the outnumbered fighter units operating in the defense of the Reich could only grow.

For the Luftwaffe, the months of February and March 1944 marked a grim chapter in its history. Pilot losses had been crippling and were no longer confined to the younger and less experienced, hurriedly trained replacements. The dilemma was now the increasing loss of experienced and virtually irreplaceable unit leaders.

Throughout April, the bomber offensive ground on, targeting aircraft factories, while Eighth Air Force fighters, as well as tactical fighters from the Ninth Air Force, began to strafe German airfields. No airspace was safe.

THE COMBATANTS

GERMAN PILOT TRAINING

The 1930s fostered a powerful sense of enthusiasm for aviation in a resurgent Germany. Thousands of young men – and many women – had been captivated by the glamor of flight. Boys grew up spellbound by the stories of Manfred von Richthofen – the famed "Red Air Fighter" and hero of the skies – and many other leading aces from World War I. This enthusiasm was fuelled further when Adolf Hitler rose to power in January 1933. Hitler recognized the tremendous propaganda and potential military value in sports flying and formed the *Nationalsozialistiches Fliegerkorps* (NSFK), a branch of the Nazi Party, to encourage boys from the age of 12 to take up flying. In line with this new "air-minded" Nazi stance, youth from all over the Reich flocked to embark on courses in fieldcraft, workshop duties, physical fitness and, ultimately, glider flying.

The career of one young man from Warstein, in Westphalia, from a flight-besotted boy to an Fw 190 *Sturmgruppe* pilot, typifies the training experienced by aspiring aviators. Willi Unger had joined his local "Flying Hitler Youth" in 1934, and here he was taught how to build and fly an elementary plywood SG 38 glider. Sufficiently competent, Unger, over the next five years, set about obtaining the required three grades of the Civil Gliding Proficiency Badge (A, B, and C) flying a Grunau Baby glider. This involved five flights of 20 seconds each and one of 30 seconds (for A), five straight and level flights of 60 seconds (for B) and a final series of more lengthy flights (for C).

In October 1939, following the outbreak of war with Poland, Unger – by now a trained machine fitter – was posted to one of many *Fliegerausbildungsregiment* where future air crew underwent basic infantry training. However, as Unger recalled,

Fw 190A-8/R2 COCKPIT

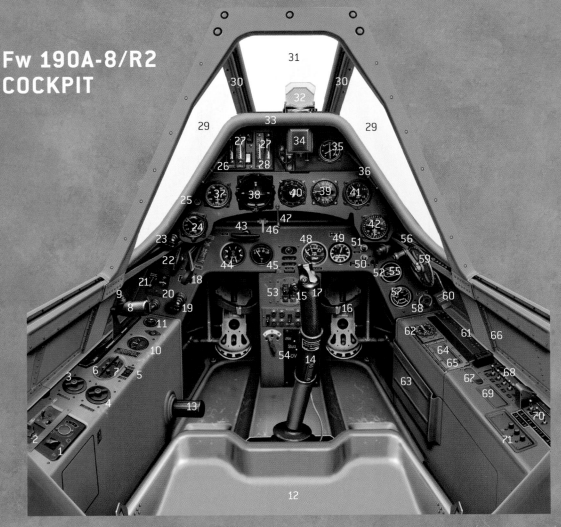

1. FuG 16ZY communication, homing switch, volume control
2. FuG 16ZY receiver fine tuning
3. FuG 16ZY homing range switch
4. FuG 16ZY frequency selector switch
5. Tailplane trim switch
6. Undercarriage and landing flap actuation buttons
7. Undercarriage and landing flap position indicators
8. Throttle
9. Throttle-mounted propeller pitch control thumb switch
10. Tailplane trim indicator
11. Panel lighting dimmer
12. Pilot's seat
13. Throttle friction knob
14. Control column
15. Bomb release button
16. Rudder pedals
17. Wing gun firing button

18. Fuel tank selector lever
19. Engine starter brushes withdrawal button
20. Stopcock control lever
21. FuG 25a IFF control panel
22. Undercarriage manual lowering handle
23. Cockpit ventilation knob
24. Altimeter
25. Pitot tube heater light
26. MG 131 armed indicator lights
27. Ammunition counters
28. SZKK 4 armament switch and control panel
29. 30mm armor glass
30. Windscreen spray pipes
31. 50mm armor glass
32. Revi 16B reflector gunsight
33. Padded coaming
34. Gunsight padded mounting
35. AFN 2 homing indicator (FuG 16ZY)

36. Ultraviolet lights (left/right)
37. Airspeed indicator
38. Artificial horizon
39. Rate of climb/descent indicator
40. Repeater compass
41. Supercharger pressure gauge
42. Tachometer
43. Ventral stores and manual release
44. Fuel and oil pressure gauge
45. Oil temperature gauge
46. Windscreen washer operating lever
47. Engine ventilation flap control lever
48. Fuel contents gauge
49. Propeller pitch indicator
50. Rear fuel tank switch-over light
51. Fuel content warning light
52. Fuel gauge selector switch

53. WGr. 21 cm underwing mortar control panel
54. Bomb fuzing selector panel and stores indicator lights
55. Oxygen flow indicator
56. Flare pistol holder
57. Oxygen pressure gauge
58. Oxygen flow valve
59. Canopy actuator drive
60. Canopy jettison lever
61. Circuit breaker panel cover
62. Clock
63. Map holder
64. Operations information card
65. Flare box cover
66. Starter switch
67. Flare box cover release knob
68. Fuel pump circuit breaker switches
69. Compass deviation card
70. Circuit breaker panel cover
71. Armament circuit breakers

WALTHER DAHL

With a recorded 678 operational missions over the Western, Eastern and Mediterranean fronts, Walther Dahl was one of the Jagdwaffe's most experienced and tenacious leaders.

Born in Lug, in the Bergzabern region of the Rheinpfalz on March 27, 1916, he joined the German Army in 1935 as an infantryman, but transferred to the Luftwaffe with the rank of leutnant on January 18, 1938. After a brief period as a flying instructor, Dahl was posted to his first operational unit, JG 3. He would see little in the way of operational flying until the early morning of June 22, 1941 when, flying a Bf 109F, he shot down a Soviet I-16 *Rata* in the opening hours of Operation *Barbarossa*, the German invasion of Russia. Although Dahl was subsequently shot down himself, he had nevertheless made one of the first claims of the campaign. After a three-day trek through enemy territory, he returned to his unit, but was subsequently transferred to II./JG 3.

On July 24, Dahl was awarded the Iron Cross 2nd Class. From then on he flew many sorties over southern Russia, and by October 23, 1941, he had accounted for 17 aircraft shot down. In early 1942, II./JG 3 was transferred for a brief spell to Sicily and attached to JG 53, from where it undertook missions against Malta. Dahl was appointed *Staffelkapitän* of 4./JG 3, but had not registered any victories in the theater before his *Gruppe* returned to Russia. He fought in the skies over Stalingrad and in the defensive fighting of December 1942–January 1943, scoring 25 victories and taking his total to 50, for which he was awarded the German Cross in Gold.

In the summer of 1943 Dahl took command of III./JG 3 following the loss of its *Kommandeur*, Major Wolfgang Ewald, over Kursk, but in early August the *Gruppe* was posted back to Münster and engaged on Reich defense duties. From here on, Dahl was to earn himself a formidable reputation as a tactical exponent in the war against the heavy bombers of the USAAF.

On March 11, Dahl was awarded the Knight's Cross in recognition of his 64 kills amongst which were nine B-17s.

In the spring of 1944, Adolf Galland, the *General der Jagdflieger*, had put forward proposals for the formation of a special *Gefechtsverband* (Battle Formation) to be known as the *Jagdgeschwader zur besonderen Verwendung* (JGzbV – Fighter Wing for Special Deployment), which would oversee a number of *Jagdgruppen* based in southern Germany that would launch quick, concentrated responses to the US bomber threat. Galland asked Dahl to lead the JGzbV, and he

enthusiastically went about his task, assembling III./JG 3, I./JG 5, II./JG 27, II./JG 53 and III./JG 54 under his command.

On May 24 the JGzbV flew its first major operation in which a successful engagement was made. Some 517 B-17s that had set out to bomb Berlin under cover of nearly 400 escort fighters were attacked. The Jagdwaffe engaged in a violent fighter-versus-fighter battle, although a few aircraft did manage to reach the bombers – the Fw 190s of III./JG 54 accounted for ten B-17s. Some 33 Fortresses were lost in total and a further 256 damaged.

Dahl was appointed *Kommodore* of JG 300 on June 6. This *Geschwader* was to subsequently play a prominent role in the war against the *Viermots*. However, despite the successes achieved with the use of close-range *Sturm* tactics in heavily armored Fw 190s, Dahl was relieved of his command by Göring on November 30, 1944 on the grounds of supposed "cowardice". By now, Dahl had been credited with 82 victories. On January 26, 1945, he was appointed *Inspekteur der Tagjäger* and was awarded the Oak Leaves to the Knight's Cross on February 1. Promoted to the rank of *oberstleutnant* at this time too, Dahl is believed to have flown the Me 262 and He 162 jet fighters in 1945.

Credited with a final total of 128 victories, including 30 confirmed (but possibly as many as 36) four-engined bombers, Dahl is ranked fourth in the list of highest-scoring "bomber-killers". He also shot down 34 Il-2 *Sturmoviks*. Finally, of his 678 missions, 300 were ground-attack.

Dahl published what is generally regarded as a colorful autobiography in 1961, and died on November 25, 1985 in Heidelberg, aged 69.

"At the beginning of the war, I was recruited into the Luftwaffe as a volunteer, but because of my profession as a machine fitter, I was assigned as an aircraft mechanic and not as a pilot – which is what I wanted to be! In spite of many applications, I only managed to become a pilot at the end of 1942."

After a frustrating delay at a technical school, Unger was finally posted to the A/B *Schule* No. 10 at Warnemünde, on the Baltic Coast. Here, he embarked on his basic pilot's flying training in aerobatics, instrument training, formation flying and cross country, making his first take-off on December 14, 1942. Between 1939 and 1942, some 1,100 pupils per month passed through such schools. In addition to further glider training, these schools used a variety of powered types including the Kl 35, Fw 44, Fw 58, Bü 131, Bü 181, He 51, Ar 96, Caudron C 445 and the W 34.

An initial instruction known as the *"Motor Auswahl"* (Powered Flight Selection) served to assess a pupil's performance, and to decide at an early stage whether he would be more suitable as a bomber or fighter pilot, or whether further training was futile.

After some 140 hours' instruction, the pupil would be given his *Führerschein* (Pilot's Badge), after which, as in Willi Unger's case, he would be posted to a *Jagdfliegerschule*, (fighter school). However, the steadily increasing rates of attrition being sustained by the Luftwaffe by the spring of 1943 placed great pressure on the training system. The *Jagdfliegerschulen* had already been redesignated as *Jagdgeschwader* during the spring of 1943. JFS 1 at Werneuchen, for example, became JG 101, where the average duration of the fighter training course was three-and-a-half to four months, compared to an average of four to five months in 1942.

Willi Unger was posted to 1./JG 104 at Fürth-Herzogenaurach under Oberleutnant Josef Unterberger. This *Staffel* was one of three forming the *"Geschwader"*, with 2. and 3.*Staffeln* at Fürth (main). 1. *Staffel* formed the *Vorschule* (Preliminary School), while 2. and 3./JG 104 formed the *Endschule* (Advanced School). Training at the *Vorschule*-level involved circuits and bumps, spot landings, turns, aerobatics, long-distance flying, navigation, diving, formation flying and some minimal awareness of battle formations and blind-flying. Students were expected to fly approximately 25 hours at the *Vorschule* on the same type of aircraft as used by the A/B schools.

The task of the *Endschule* was to prepare and convert the pupil onto either the Bf 109 or Fw 190 in a series of circuits and bumps in dual-control aircraft, followed by ten solo flights, then formation practise in pairs and fours, followed by a high-altitude flight with oxygen, a practise flight concentrating on weak points and culminating in two firing training flights, each comprising three approaches to a ground target. This covered another 16–18 hours.

Reductions in the training program meant that by the autumn of 1943, fighter pilots were reaching their operational units with an average of 148 hours on powered aircraft spread across an elementary A/B school, a *Jagdfliegerschule* and an Operational Fighter Training "Pool" or *Ergänzungsjagdgruppe*. This was down from an average of 210 hours the previous year.

In June 1943, the four component *Staffeln* of *Ergänzungsjagdgruppe West,* spread across southwestern France, supplied Bf 109- and Fw 190-ready pilots to operational *Jagdgruppen.* Pupils were instructed by operationally experienced instructors over courses lasting normally one month, though demands from the operational units often shortened this period to 14 days. Courses consisted of circuits and bumps in an Bf 108 prior to conversion to the Fw 190. Instruction in formation flying was similar to that received in a *Jagdfliegerschule,* but in an *Ergänzungsjagdgruppe,* at least one flight was made in a formation of seven to nine aircraft led by an instructor. Heavy emphasis was placed on gunnery training and target practise, using both machine gun and cannon.

Following two months in France with 2./*Ergänzungsjagdgruppe Ost* at La Leu, near Rochelle, in January–February 1944, Willi Unger was finally posted to his operational unit, 11./JG 3, on March 10, 1944, where he would fly both the Bf 109G-6 and Fw 190A-8 in combat. However, from this point on, an increasing Allied campaign of low-level attacks on German airfields, a resulting state of alert and a general feeling of insecurity badly interrupted training at all levels. During April and May 1944, no fewer than 67 Luftwaffe aircraft were shot down during training, transfer or travel flights over Reich territory.

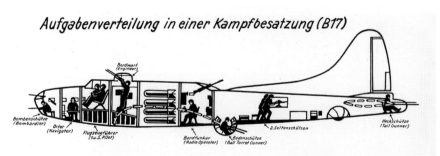

A page from a Luftwaffe tactical manual showing the crew and gun positions in a B-17F. It was vital for German fighter pilots to be familiar with the layout, strengths and weaknesses of their opposition. Armed with such information, optimum tactics could be devised that would ensure maximum success with minimum risk.

B-17G FLYING FORTRESS
CHEYENNE TAIL TURRET

1. Gunsight
2. Bullet-proof glass shield
3. Hand grips for twin 0.50-in. Browning M-2 machine guns
4. Light
5. Defrost tubes for Plexiglas
6. Interphone jack

7. Oxygen regulator
8. Oxygen gauges
9. Oxygen hoses
10. Interphone jack box
11. Oxygen supply
12. 0.50-in. ammunition boxes
13. 0.50-in. ammunition feed belts

14. Gunner's seat and seat belts
15. Gunner's knee pads
16. Heated flight suit electrical outlet
17. Portable oxygen bottle
18. Switch panel
19. Wooden catwalk

As the economic and military infrastructure of the Reich became directly threatened by the burgeoning Allied air offensive, Generalleutnant Josef Schmid, commander of the I. *Jagdkorps* which controlled day fighter tactical deployment in the *Reichsverteidigung*, described the condition of the *Jagdwaffe* at this time:

"Heavy losses, as well as the great physical and psychological strain imposed on German fighter pilots, reduced the combat value of our units in April and May 1944. The young replacements showed deficiencies in flying and radio usage. They lacked combat experience, particularly in respect to high-altitude operations. Time and opportunities for training in the operational units was lacking to an increasing extent. The shortage of qualified formation leaders increased. The excessive strain caused by almost uninterrupted commitment resulted in combat fatigue. Experienced fighter pilots reached the limit of their efficiency."

For Willi Unger, and hundreds of other freshly qualified fighter pilots, it was merely a portent of things to come.

USAAF AIR GUNNERY TRAINING

Before the appearance of P-47s with drop tanks from the autumn of 1943, and later P-51s, which could escort B-17s to deep penetration targets in Germany, the Flying Fortress' defense was its guns, and their correct use was vital to the survival of air crew when under fighter attack. This was illustrated in stark terms by the Las Vegas Army Air Field (LVAAF) Year Book of the same year, which recorded the role of the gunner:

"Protection they provide is vital to success of long-range bombing. On this ability of self-protection, long-range bombing is built. Each bomber, alone, must be able to

For German fighter pilots flying in the defense of the Reich in mid-1943, there was little opportunity to forget the number one target. Here, the formidable frontal view of a B-17F has been painted in scale on the doors of a hangar for range training purposes.

hold its own against fighters. Everything depends on the ability of one special class of men, the aerial gunners. They have to be good or they are dead, and heavy bombardment is dead with them. The five men who handle the guns in a bomber crew of nine are trained as mechanics, radio operators, cameramen. Many of them have never fired a gun. In order to make them first-rate gunners, the Air Forces give them the toughest six weeks of training in the Army.

"At the special schools, they learn their deadly business. Taught precision on miniature ranges with 0.22-cal rifles, they learn to lead and swing while shooting trap and skeet. They fire machine guns, find out the trick of the turrets, have special training on altitude flying, and when their course is finished they are assigned to operational training units ready for combat.

"If straws point to the wind, Las Vegas Air Field is one straw in the Nation's military program, and progress that bespeaks a storm of trouble and discomfort for the enemy."

This self-belief was neither ill-founded, nor exaggerated. At the beginning of the war, the USAAC had no training facilities for aerial gunnery, but in the summer of 1941, a group of officers was sent to England to seek guidance on how to set up such a school. Subsequently, future B-17 air gunners would arrive at the Flexible Gunnery School north of Las Vegas, which provided training in moveable, as opposed to fixed, guns of the type to be found on a heavy bomber. The first thing that struck most trainees arriving at the base was the searing heat and the inhospitable Nevada landscape. As one man recalled, "All you can see is desert sand and mountains, mile upon mile."

Here, future gunners would practice using air rifles for marksmanship, shooting at clay pigeons on the ground and from moving trucks, before firing machine guns on the ground. The student then graduated to the ground turret, firing machine guns at towed flags. Finally, they would fire in the air from B-34s and B-26s. Most of the course was dedicated to the 0.50-in. Browning M-2, which was the weapon gunners would use in the skies over Europe. Trainees were taught how to strip a gun down and then – under test conditions – reassemble the 80 or so parts blindfolded.

When about two-thirds of the way through the course, trainees were transferred to another facility in the same state at Indian Springs, where there would be a brief period of airborne gunnery training on AT-6 Texans using ammunition filled with different-colored paint to assess individual accuracy and scoring. Finally, they would return to Las Vegas and be introduced to the B-17.

On average, during the second half of World War II, 600 gunnery students graduated from the LVAAF every five weeks, although during 1943 the school graduated 9,117 gunners. By September 1944, 227,827 gunners had been trained.

So it was that upon transfer to the ETO, gunners *seemed* highly skilled, and knew their aircraft inside and out. Initially, however, it had not been easy in England. The truth was that general standards of nose and waist position air gunnery were poor – despite high claims made during the initial clashes with the Luftwaffe – and incidents of damage from friendly fire were not uncommon. The effective use of a heavy, reverberating 0.50-in. machine gun in a 200mph slipstream against a small, fast-moving target presented enormous challenges.

Following the arrival of the first bomb groups from the US in 1942, Eaker and VIII BC set up further intensive gunnery training courses on land and coastal ranges procured from the British, such as those near Snettisham and in Cornwall, and by acquiring a handful of target-towing aircraft. Nevertheless, the overall standard of air gunnery remained disappointing for the rest of the year.

THE GUNNERS

The B-17 is a most effective gun platform, but its effectiveness can be either applied or defeated by the way the gunners in your crew perform their duties in action.

Your gunners belong to one of two distinct categories: turret gunners and flexible gunners.

The power turret gunners require many mental and physical qualities similar to what we know as inherent flying ability, since the operation of the power turret and gunsight are much like that of airplane flight operation.

While the flexible gunners do not require the same delicate touch as the turret gunner, they must have a fine sense of timing and be familiar with the rudiments of exterior ballistics.

All gunners should be familiar with the coverage area of all gun positions, and be prepared to bring the proper gun to bear as the conditions may warrant.

They should be experts in aircraft identification. Where the Sperry turret is used, failure to set the target dimension dial properly on the K-type sight will result in miscalculation of range.

They must be thoroughly familiar with the Browning aircraft machine gun. They should know how to maintain the guns, how to clear jams and stoppages, and how to harmonize the sights with the guns.

While participating in training flights, the gunners should be operating their turrets constantly, tracking with the flexible guns even when actual firing is not practical. Other airplanes flying in the vicinity offer excellent tracking targets, as do automobiles, houses, and other ground objects during low altitude flights.

The importance of teamwork cannot be overemphasized. One poorly trained gunner, or one man not on the alert, can be the weak link as a result of which the entire crew may be lost.

Keep the interest of your gunners alive at all times. Any form of competition among the gunners themselves should stimulate interest to a high degree.

Finally, each gunner should fire the guns at each station to familiarize himself with the other man's position and to insure knowledge of operation in the event of an emergency.

A page from a 1944 B-17 pilot training manual.

Even as late as November 1944, the Eighth Air Force conceded that "There appears to be a serious weakness in nose gunnery. This is seen in the steady growth of the percentage of nose attacks, since enemy fighters may be expected to attack weak spots. There are explanations of this weakness: (1) the navigators and bombardiers have other primary duties, and tend to neglect their duty as gunners; (2) a high percentage of the navigators and bombardiers have had no gunnery training whatsoever."

However, by the time new B-17 groups arrived in numbers in England for the Eighth Air Force during the winter of 1943–44, operational training had reached considerably higher standards in the US. Much of it was handled by Combat Crew Replacement Centers (CCRC), although ad hoc forms of training continued to be meted out at unit level. In April 1944, inventive gunnery officers at Kimbolton, for example, constructed their own timber rig in a blister hangar into which were fitted chin, ball and top turrets and nose gun positions from wrecked B-17s. Target images were then projected into a screen, while elsewhere on the airfield a B-17 top turret was fitted onto the back of a truck. The latter would then be driven along a perimeter track and the new gunner would practice his aim against friendly aircraft flying over the airfield.

KERMIT D. STEVENS

One of the Eighth Air Force's most experienced staff operations officers and group commanders, Kermit D. Stevens was born in Roseburg, Oregon, on December 16, 1908. He embarked upon his first military service as a Reserve Officers' Training Corps (ROTC) student at the University of Oregon, from where he graduated with a BS degree. Stevens entered the Army Air Corps as a flying cadet in 1935, and was commissioned the following year at Kelly Field, in Texas. For four years thereafter he served with the 3rd Attack Group, which was eventually equipped with A-20 Havocs. Rising to the rank of squadron commander, Stevens eventually joined the Eighth Air Force upon its formation at Savannah Army Air Base, in Georgia, in late January 1942.

Soon after, Stevens journeyed to England as a member of one of the first command staffs to arrive at the fledgling Eighth Air Force's new headquarters at Daws Hill Lodge, a country house in High Wycombe, Buckinghamshire.

He served with the Eighth Air Force as an operations officer until transferring to the 303rd BG (H), based at Molesworth in Huntingdonshire, as group Commanding Officer on July 19, 1943, taking over from Col Charles E. Marion. Stevens then began an illustrious career with the "Hell's Angels", leading the group on many successful missions to Germany, amongst them Huls, Schweinfurt, Frankfurt, Bremen, Cologne, Berlin-Erkner and Hamburg.

On August 16, 1943, just under a month after having assumed command, Stevens led 20 of the 303rd BG's B-17s to Le Bourget airfield in France, during which he piloted B-17F 42-5431 *Vicious Virgin* of the 427th BS. Ball turret gunner Sgt Frank Garret participated in this mission in B-17F 41-24605 *Knockout Dropper*, and he later commented, "Followed those bombs all the way down and they really smacked the place. Shot at plenty of fighters." Stevens, on the other hand, commented somewhat laconically, "Left a lot of smoke down there. We blew a few

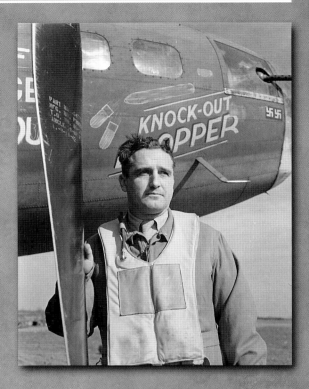

people's hats off anyway", and was duly awarded the Silver Star for Gallantry for his conduct during this highly successful raid.

Stevens relinquished command of the 303rd BG on September 1, 1944. It subsequently became the first Eighth Air Force bomb group to complete 300 missions from the UK, and ultimately flew more missions than any other B-17 outfit, and was beaten by just one other unit in dropping more bomb tonnage. In November of that year, while on leave in the United States, Stevens was appointed CO of a B-29 training field that was operating as part of the Second Air Force.

Col Stevens retired from the US Air Force on January 31, 1964 and lived in California. He died on November 21, 2004.

COMBAT

TACTICS

Commencing summer 1942, B-17 Flying Fortresses began attacking targets in occupied France and, from January 1943, in Germany too. Luftwaffe tacticians quickly realized that it was no mean feat to bring down just one heavily armed *Viermot*. Breaking through a fighter escort in an Fw 190 so as to get close enough to the bombers to ensure success was a difficult and draining task. German pilots would usually resort to making a solitary high-speed diving pass through the ranks of the escorting fighters, firing their weapons at the nearest bomber and then seeking refuge in cloud, followed by a quick return to base.

As the range of the raids increased and the escort reduced, so the Luftwaffe invariably attacked from the rear of a formation. Such a method resulted in heavy losses incurred from the bombers' intense rearward defensive fire, however. This in turn meant that the *Jagdflieger* were often reluctant to press home an attack to close range, opening fire only at extreme, and thus ineffective, distances of around 1,000m.

From the American point of view, in a revealing report prepared for the British Air Ministry in September 1942, a USAAF liaison officer wrote:

This formation of B-17s appears to have lost its cohesion, and the aircraft may well be returning from a mission with depleted ranks.

"Our gunners are given sectors to search so that all fields of view are covered. At least three guns may be brought to bear on any point 400 yards from a B-17F. Mutual firepower from ships in formation greatly increases the number of guns that may fire at enemy aircraft attacking the formation.

"Enemy fighter attacks from all angles have been experienced. They started with stern attacks, then went to quarter, beam, below, bow and, on the last two missions, head-on attacks. The success of all these attacks has been about the same. The B-17s that have been shot down have been from the usual causes of straggling and gunners getting killed. Damage to airplanes returning has been slight, and there have only been two airplanes at any one time out of commission due to enemy gunfire. Gunners have caused many fighters to decide not to attack by firing a burst just as the fighter begins the turn-in to attack. This has been done on some occasions when the fighter was 1,000 yards away or more."

An Fw 190 firing a three-second burst loosed off some 130 rounds from each set of guns. It was generally recognized that 20 rounds of 20mm cannon fire were required to shoot down a bomber, unless a shell managed to hit a sensitive area of the aircraft such as the wing fuel tanks. Analysis of gun-camera films led German tacticians and armament experts to believe that the average fighter pilot scored hits on a bomber with only some two percent of the total number of rounds fired. Thus, to obtain the necessary 20 rounds for a "kill", 1,000 rounds of 20mm ammunition would need to be expended over a 23-second firing pass in a Fw 190A-4 – a dangerously long period for a rear-mounted attack.

On November 23, 1942, a force of 36 unescorted B-17s and B-24s attacked the St Nazaire U-boat base. As the B-17s made their bomb run, Fw 190s from Hauptmann Egon Mayer's III./JG 2 swept in to meet them. The attack provided Mayer with the perfect opportunity to test a new tactic that had been the subject of discussion among German fighter commanders for several weeks. Forming into *Ketten* of three aircraft, the Fw 190s went into the attack from dead-ahead, and at speed,

before firing a no-deflection burst and breaking away in a climb or half-roll beneath the bombers. Mayer believed that a frontal pass, as opposed to the customary rearward attack, offered the best chance of hitting the bombers' vulnerable cockpit area. Even more importantly, the B-17's frontal arc of defensive fire was the weakest. Four bombers went down following the attack for the loss of only one Fw 190. "From that moment", one historian recorded, "the B-17 was obsolete as a self-defending bomber."

Encouraged by this success, Generalmajor Galland issued the following circular to all Luftwaffe fighter units:

"A.) The attack from the rear against a four-engined bomber formation promises little success and almost always brings losses. If an attack from the rear must be carried through, it should be done from above or below, and the fuel tanks and engines should be the aiming points.

"B.) The attack from the side can be effective, but it requires thorough training and good gunnery.

"C.) The attack from the front, front high or front low, all with low speed, is the most effective of all. Flying ability, good aiming and closing up to the shortest possible range are the prerequisites for success. Basically, the strongest weapon is the massed and repeated attack by an entire fighter formation. In such cases, the defensive fire can be weakened and the bomber formation broken up."

The air war over Europe intensified during the first half of 1943. Yet German tactics seemed to sway between attacks from the rear and from head-on. Those pilots persisting in rearward attacks found that the most vulnerable spot on a bomber was the wing area between the fuselage and the in-board engines. The No 3 engine on a B-17 was considered particularly important because it powered the hydraulic system.

When necessary, in executing the head-on attack, the cockpit and the No 3 engine became the key targets. However, in August 1943, the *Oberkommando der Luftwaffe* (OKL, Luftwaffe High Command) ordered that all attacks must be made from the rear once again, rather than by a frontal pass, chiefly because a large percentage of the young, inexperienced pilots now equipping the *Jagdgeschwader* encountered difficulty in undertaking the latter type of attack. The frontal pass involved a high combined closing speed which, in turn, demanded great skill in gunnery, range estimation and flying control. The slightest evasive action on the part of the bombers made this type of attack even more difficult. In contrast, evasive action taken against attacks from the rear was thought ineffective.

ABOVE
Major Egon Mayer of III./JG 2 stands next to his Fw 190A-4 or A-5 in northwest France in early 1943. The rudder is decorated with 62 victories, including the marks for six four-engined bombers, of which five were B-17s — two were shot down on November 23, 1942 and two on January 3, 1943. Mayer would receive the Swords to his Knight's Cross posthumously following his death in action over Montmédy on March 2, 1944. He had downed 102 enemy aircraft, including 21 B-17s.

LEFT
Luftwaffe ace Egon Mayer believed that a frontal pass, as opposed to the customary rearward attack against heavy bombers, offered the best chance to inflict damage on the vulnerable cockpit area of a B-17. Even more importantly, the frontal arc of defensive fire was the weakest.

RIGHT
Under a hail of gun fire, a B-17 falls away from formation with one engine already on fire during an Fw 190 attack over Germany in March 1944.

53

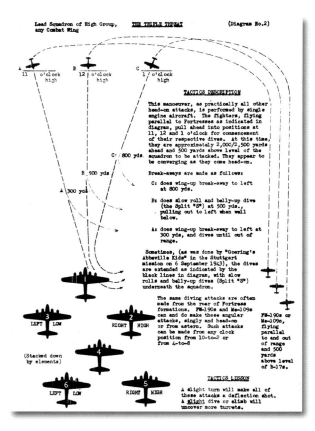

A   11 o'clock high   B   12 o'clock high   C   1 o'clock high

C: 800 yds.

B: 500 yds

A: 300 yds

TACTICS DESCRIPTION

This manoeuvre, as practically all other head-on attacks, is performed by single engine aircraft. The fighters, flying parallel to Fortresses as indicated in diagram, pull ahead into positions at 11, 12 and 1 o'clock for commencement of their respective dives. At this time, they are approximately 2,000/2,500 yards ahead and 500 yards above level of the squadron to be attacked. They appear to be converging as they come head-on.

Break-aways are made as follows:

C: does wing-up break-away to left at 800 yds.

B: does slow roll and belly-up dive (the Split "S") at 500 yds., pulling out to left when well below.

A: does wing-up break-away to left at 300 yds, and dives until out of range.

Sometimes, (as was done by "Goering's Abbeville Kids" in the Stuttgart mission on 6 September 1943), the dives are extended as indicated by the black lines in diagram, with slow rolls and belly-up dives (Split "S") underneath the squadron.

The same diving attacks are often made from the rear of Fortress formations. FW-190s and Me-109s can and do make these angular attacks, singly and head-on or from astern. Such attacks can be made from any clock position from 10-to-2 or from 4-to-8.

3 LEFT LOW   2 RIGHT HIGH

(Stacked down by elements)

4

6 LEFT LOW   5 RIGHT HIGH

FW-190s or Me-109s, flying parallel to and out of range and 500 yards above level of B-17s.

TACTICS LESSON

A slight turn will make all of these attacks a deflection shot. A slight dive or climb will uncover more turrets.

One of a series of diagrams produced by the US 3rd Bombardment Division in November 1943 showing types of attack mounted by German fighters against the its B-17s. This diagram shows the "Triple Threat", whereby three Fw 190s attack from the front at the 11, 12 and 1 o'clock high positions. The division noted that, "The Hun is an opportunist, and is quick to change his approach if he can get in a better shot." Other forms of attack were given such colorful descriptions as "The Rocketeers", "The Roller Coaster", "The Sisters Act", "The Swooper" and "The Single Engine Tail Pecker"!

The reversion to rear-mounted attacks proved to be timely, for September 1943 saw the appearance of the new B-17G fitted with a Bendix twin-gun chin turret. This provided the Fortress with the vital forward armament it needed to counter frontally mounted attacks.

At this point the battle escalated, with new types of weapon being deployed that were intended specifically for use against the "heavies". Fw 190s of JGs 1 and 11 carried 21cm Werfergranate mortar tubes (or "stovepipes") under their wings. Originally, designed as an infantry weapon, the mortar was to be fired from beyond the defensive range of the bombers. However, the blast effect from a shell exploding within the confines of a formation, or even just near to it, would scatter the *Viermots*, thus weakening their defensive firepower and rendering individual bombers more vulnerable to attack. In a report prepared in late August 1943, the Eighth Air Force warned, "It would appear to be the most dangerous single obstacle in the path of our bomber offensive." The weapon was perhaps used to its greatest effect against the raid on Schweinfurt on October 14, 1943, when 62 bombers were downed, many as a result of being dispersed from their formations by the use of the mortar.

During the autumn of 1943 came an "innovator" in the form of Major Hans-Günter von Kornatzki, a member of Galland's staff, who, in a response to the bomber threat, proposed the formation of a specially equipped *Sturmstaffel*. Kornatzki advocated radical new tactics involving massed rear attacks by tight formations of heavily armed and armored Fw 190s. Having studied gun camera film, read combat reports describing attacks on *Viermots* and interviewed pilots, Kornatzki reasoned that during a rearward attack against an American formation, one German fighter was exposed to the defensive fire of more than 40 0.50-in. Browning M-2s, resulting in only the slimmest chance of escaping damage during attack. Under such circumstances it was even less likely that a lone fighter could bring down a bomber.

However, if a complete *Gruppe* could position itself for an attack at close range, the bomber gunners would be forced to disperse their fire, and thus weaken it, allowing individual fighters greater opportunity to close in, avoid damage and shoot a bomber down. The loss of speed and manoeuvrability incurred by the extra armament and armor carried by these *Sturm* aircraft would be countered by the presence of two regular fighter *Gruppen*, whose job it would be to keep any escort fighters at bay.

Kornatzki also suggested that as a last-ditch resort, when pilots were close enough and if ammunition had been expended, a bomber could be rammed in order to bring it

Armorers load a 152kg WGr. 21cm mortar shell into a firing tube beneath the wing of an Fw 190A-8/R6 of *Stab*/JG 26 in the summer of 1944. Despite a direct hit by one of these shells on a bomber being devastating, and just the weapon's blast effect being sufficient to break up a bomber formation, the results achieved with the mortar were debatable, as German fighter pilots tended to fire them from too great a range.

B-17F *Sad Sack* of the 379th BG suffered a direct hit from a 21cm shell during the July 28, 1943 mission to Kassel and Oschersleben, but the bomber survived to return to England. Struck below the top turret, large shell fragments exploded the aircraft's oxygen bottles, which in turn blasted a large hole in the forward fuselage.

down. It seems that Adolf Galland needed little convincing. He immediately authorized the establishment of *Sturmstaffel* 1 and appointed Major Kornatzki its commander.

On November 8, 1943, the *General der Jagdflieger* signalled his unit commanders:

"German fighters have been unable to obtain decisive successes in the defense against American four-engined formations. Even the introduction of new weaponry has not appreciably changed the situation. The main reason for this is the failure of formation leaders to lead up whole formations for attack at the closest possible range. Göring has therefore ordered the establishment of a *Sturmstaffel*, whose task will be to break up Allied formations by means of an all-out attack with more heavily armed

Major Hans-Günter von Kornatzki studied reels of gun camera films and many combat reports. He reasoned that a mass attack made from the rear of a bomber formation would ensure less damage to German fighters, and offer a pilot a greater chance of shooting a *Viermot* down. Born on June 22, 1906 in Liegnitz, Kornatzki served in the *Reichswehr* from 1928. He entered the Luftwaffe in 1933 and trained as a pilot in 1934, before serving in II./JG 132, JG 334 and I./JG 136. Kornatzki was appointed *Kommandeur* of II./JG 52 in September 1939, and then became chief instructor at *Jagdfliegerschule* 1. On May 3, 1941, Kornatzki married a secretary to Reichsmarschall Göring and the daughter of a generalmajor. After the disbanding of *Sturmstaffel* 1, he became *Kommandeur* of II.(*Sturm*)/JG 4, but Kornatzki was killed in an Fw 190A-8 by American fighters on September 12, 1944, holding the rank of *oberstleutnant*. He had just shot down a B-17.

fighters in close formation and at the closest range. Such attacks that are undertaken are to be pressed home to the very heart of the Allied formation whatever happens, and without regard to losses, until the formation is annihilated."

By then *Sturmstaffel* 1 had already received its first complement of Fw 190A-6s with 30mm armored glass panels – or *Panzerscheiben* – fitted around the standard glass cockpit side panels and a 5mm plate of strengthened glass that would protect the pilot from fire from dead ahead. External 5mm steel plates to the fuselage panelling around the cockpit and the nose–cockpit join offered further protection from defensive fire. Additionally, the pilot's seat was fortified by 5mm steel plates and a 12mm head protection panel.

Pilots of *Sturmstaffel* 1 were made to swear the following oath:

"1.) I volunteer for the *Sturmstaffel* of my own free will.

"A.) Without exception, the enemy will be approached in close formation.

"B.) Losses during the approach will be immediately made up by closing up with the attack leader.

"C.) The enemy will be shot down at the closest range. If that becomes impossible, ramming will be the only alternative.

"D.) The *Sturm* pilot will remain with the damaged bomber until the aircraft impacts.

"2.) I voluntarily take up an obligation to carry out these tactics, and will not land until the enemy has crashed. If these fundamentals are violated, I will face a court martial or will be removed from the unit."

Historically, the Americans had favored an 18-aircraft "combat box" formation of B-17s, comprised of three six-aircraft squadrons, each broken down into two three-aircraft flights. Succeeding "combat boxes" of a similar composition trailed in one-and-a-half-mile breaks behind the lead box.

By late 1943, however, in a measure intended to stiffen defensive firepower and increase protection, bombing formations were usually made up of a 36-aircraft box. This formation, similarly composed of squadrons of six aircraft broken into two elements of three aircraft, had developed from attempts to concentrate as many aircraft together to take advantage of the relatively few radar Pathfinders available at that time. All aircraft in an element flew at the same level, but the elements themselves were separated in altitude by a little stagger, forming into high, low and "low-low" positions.

These combat boxes then formed a bomber column, with groups in trail, each flying at the same altitude and separated by some four miles. Such a formation was more suited to "blind" bombing, and it was also easier for fighters to escort since it was a more "disciplined" structure than had been used before. But, as with all large formations, it was difficult to hold.

By the winter of 1943–44, combat attrition (losses, as well as aircraft grounded with battle damage and in need of repair) caused by German fighters attacking *en masse* often compelled the Eighth Air Force to despatch combat boxes reduced from 36 to just 18 or 21 aircraft.

One of the first Fw 190A-6s to be delivered to *Sturmstaffel* 1 runs up its engine at Achmer or Dortmund in the autumn of 1943/early 1944. The canopy has armored quarter panels installed, and there is cockpit side armor fitted to the fuselage. The aircraft carries the lightning and gauntlet emblem of the *Staffel*, as well as the unit's black-white-black fuselage identification band.

By March 1944, a typical 21-aircraft box comprised three squadrons, each of two elements – the lead squadron with six aircraft, the low squadron with six and the high squadron with nine. The high and low squadrons flew on opposite sides of the lead, forming a "V" pointing in the direction of flight and tilted to 45 degrees. The spacing of individual bombers in a box (usually 100–200ft, which was the equivalent of between one and two wingspans) maximized collective firepower but minimized the risks of unwieldiness, interference with bomb runs and buffeting and displacement from slipstream.

When fully assembled, a bomber stream could stretch for 90 miles, presenting a problem for the escort fighters, which had to zigzag to compensate for the bombers' lower speeds. Furthermore, individual fighter groups were not able to stay with the bombers for much more than 30 minutes before fuel ran low, which meant that only a small number of escorts covered the bombers at any one time. It was normal that a third of the escort flew "up front" to cover the head of the bomber stream and protect it from a head-on attack.

Leutnant Richard Franz of *Sturmstaffel* 1 recalls what it was like to target a bomber:

"At this time, the *Sturmstaffel* was the only unit in the Luftwaffe that attacked bombers from the rear, flying a 'V' formation. The close 'V' formation provided a very strong attacking force with extreme firepower, so that when we engaged we were always successful. On the one hand, unlike the usual head-on tactic, this gave us much more time to attack and shoot, but on the other hand, the Fortress gunners had the same advantage. In my opinion – and as I recall – the defensive bomber formation was very effective, because in trying to attack it, it was very difficult to find even one angle from which you were not subject to defensive fire."

The disbandment of *Sturmstaffel* 1 at the end of April 1944 did not signify the Luftwaffe's abandoning Kornatzki's philosophy. To the contrary. Encouraged by the results achieved in such a short time by such a small unit, OKL decided to establish two new *Sturmgruppen*, II.(*Sturm*)/JG 4 and II.(*Sturm*)/JG 300, in addition to the newly designated IV.(*Sturm*)/JG 3.

The standard USAAF Combat Wing formation fielded 54 B-17s (sometimes mixed with B-24s) in three "boxes" of bombers (in high, lead and low positions), each consisting of three six-aircraft squadrons echeloned into lead, high and low. In turn, the squadrons were formed of two three-ship flights (high and low). Such a formation, despite requiring considerable assembly time and disciplined flight control, ensured a high level of mutual protection and defense, although the bombers flying in the second flights of the low squadrons were most vulnerable – they were a favorite target for rear-mounted attacks by Fw 190s. Nevertheless, the prospect of attacking such a formation – even without escort – was a daunting prospect.

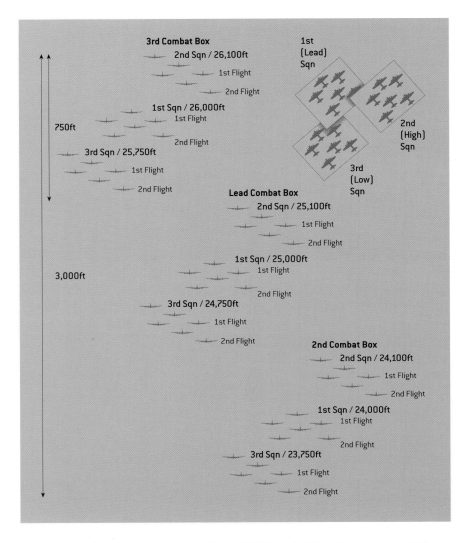

The recently appointed commander of IV.(*Sturm*)/JG 3, Hauptmann Wilhelm Moritz, recalled, "For my part, I never accepted the fighting tactic favored by Kornatzki and never bound a pilot to ram a bomber. My IV./JG 3 scored many victories attacking bombers with traditional tactics, and their successes rested on the sense of duty and the tactics of my men – namely, attacking in closed formation and opening fire at close quarters."

Perhaps the most immediate change for the *Gruppe*, however, was the replacement of its Bf 109G-6s with the more heavily armed, and armored, Fw 190A-8 *Sturmjäger*, which carried two 30mm MK 108s in the wings. Feldwebel Willi Unger of 11.(*Sturm*)/JG 3 summarized the Fw 190A-8 thus:

"Advantages – wide undercarriage, large twin-row radial engine which protected the pilot from fire from the front, electric starter motor and electric trim system. Disadvantages – there was a danger of turning over when braking hard on soft or sandy ground. In combat against enemy fighters, more awkward because of the heavy armor plating. Strong at low altitude, inferior to the Bf 109 at higher altitude. In my opinion, the Fw 190, in this version, was the best aircraft used in formation against the *Viermots*."

Richard Franz remembered:

"When we made our attack, we approached from slightly above, then dived, opening fire with 13mm and 20mm guns to knock out the rear gunner and then, at about 150m, we tried to engage with the MK 108 30mm cannon, which was a formidable weapon. It could cut off the wing of a B-17. Actually, it was still easier to kill a B-24, which was somewhat weaker in respect of fuselage strength and armament. I think that we generally had the better armament and ammunition, whereas the other side had the better aircraft."

Unteroffizier Oscar Boesch, a young Austrian pilot who served with *Sturmstaffel* 1 and IV.(*Sturm*)/JG 3, recalled:

"The bomber gunners usually started to fire and waste their ammunition while we were still out of range at 2,000m from them. It was obvious that they were just as scared as we were. Shaken by the slipstream of the B-17s and blinded by condensation trails, we were subjected to machine gun fire for minutes or seconds that seemed endless before being able to see the results of our attack. Despite the armor plating of our cockpits, we had good reason to dread the defensive fire of the bombers.

"We always went in in line abreast. If you went in singly, all the bombers shot at you with their massive defensive firepower. But as an attack formation, the psychological effect on the bomber gunners was much greater. First of all you tried to knock out the tail gunner. Then you went for the intersection between wing and fuselage, and you just kept at it, watching your hits flare and flare again. It all happened so quick. You gave it all you had.

"Sometimes, after the first attack, all your energy seemed to go. Your nerves were burned out. But we had this kind of theory that when you were in the middle of a bomber formation – flying through it – you were, in a way, 'protected'. The bombers wouldn't open fire because they didn't want to shoot at their own aircraft. We would break off the attack just before we were about to collide with our target. The devastating effect of our 30mm cannon was such that we would often fly

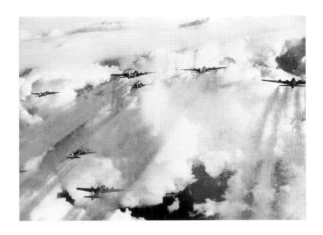

The Fw 190s of *Sturmstaffel* 1 would usually mount a massed attack from above and behind a bomber formation, such as the one seen here en route to Bremen in late 1943. Leutnant Richard Franz, who flew with the *Staffel*, remembered, "We tried to engage the enemy with the MK 108 cannon, which was a formidable weapon. It could cut off the wing of a B-17."

through a rain of fragments, some being complete sections of aircraft."

Major Anton Hackl, *Gruppenkommandeur* of III./JG 11, wore the Oak Leaves to the Knight's Cross, and with more than 150 victories to his credit he was one of the Luftwaffe's principal tacticians and a leading "bomber killer". On May 20, 1944, he sent a paper to Galland in which he offered his suggestions on what was required to deal with the *Viermots*:

"The aim of all fighter formations in operations against bombers should be to attack as late as possible, causing bombers to jettison their ordnance, even though a late approach excludes the possibility of a second operation, or to attack as early as possible, thus allowing *Gruppe* after *Gruppe* to attack at minute intervals.

"Firstly, Allied fighter relief would then be forced to deal with the main body of attacking elements one after the other, necessitating a splitting of forces that would leave it out of position to hamper individual *Gruppen* making repeated frontal attacks, even where there was Allied high-altitude fighter cover.

"Secondly, when flying a follow-up sortie, auxiliary tanks should be retained as far as possible so as to challenge formations as deep as possible inside the Reich. Fighter protection is less bold and weaker here, and relief does not always arrive as scheduled.

"Thirdly, it is certainly possible to break up formations through these tactics. Rear attacks are then possible so that even bad gunners would have to get a victory or be suspected of cowardice. Experience of frontal attacks show that only older (experienced) pilots get victories and, for the most part, they get hit too. Younger pilots do not approach correctly, nor go in near enough.

"Fourthly, my *Gruppe* proposes therefore 1) to bring over continually from the Russian Front young pilots with few victories so that the East would become a kind of battle school for the West, and 2) every pilot, even when his ammunition has been expended, must attack in formation as long as the *Kommandeur* does, in order to split up defense and prevent our own pilots refusing combat."

In a report compiled during the summer of 1944, Eighth Air Force analysts confessed "Even extensive escort cover cannot prevent a relatively small but determined enemy force from avoiding, or swamping, the cover and attacking the bombers at some point in the long formation."

On May 29, 1944, 993 bombers of the Eighth Air Force attacked aircraft industry targets, an oil terminal and airfields in central Germany. This force was escorted by a record 1,265 fighters. B-17G 42-31924 *Ol' Dog* was one of 251 bombers from the 3rd BD which was assigned to attack aircraft plants at Leipzig. An aircraft of the 344th BS/95th BG, based at Horham in Suffolk, *Ol' Dog* was embarking on its 41st mission, and was piloted by 2Lt Norman A. Ulrich.

The B-17s of the 1st and 3rd BDs formed up over East Anglia and left the British coast from Cromer and Great Yarmouth, tracking across the North Sea towards the

Zuider Zee on course for Hannover. The navigator on board *Ol' Dog* was 2Lt Ralph W Smithberger, who recalled:

"*Ol' Dog* took off at 0600hrs that Monday without a problem. The squadron and wing assembled in proper formation as we approached the Channel. During this time, I checked my maps and charts. While over the Channel, I test-fired my two guns and our bombardier, 2Lt Don Payne, did the same with the chin turret guns. You could hear the clatter of 'fifties' throughout the airplane as all of our gunners followed suit. The crew was really tired because we had flown a maximum effort mission to Dessau the day before, and today was another big mission. We didn't get much sleep the night before these deep penetration missions."

To intercept the bombers, the Luftwaffe readied 275 single- and twin-engined fighters, most of which were placed on 15 minutes' readiness at 0815hrs.

Towards midday, the B-17s of the 3rd BD were nearing their target when the low groups of the 2nd and 4th CBWs were attacked by "40 to 60" German fighters in a series of frontal and rear attacks whilst the escort was not present. For the crew of *Ol' Dog*, a nightmare was about to begin, as Ulrich explained:

"Flying formation was total monotony. We saw fighters far off in the distance and wondered if they were ours or theirs. Suddenly, over the intercom, I heard 'Fighters at ten o'clock', and when I looked out the window I could see them in front of us. They were coming at us, and fast! Within seconds of this sighting, the world exploded and total monotony became total terror. I remember two Fw 190s coming at us, but one in particular seemed to have us in his sights with his cannon blazing away. I could feel the impact of his shells hitting our airplane, but at the same time I saw the Fw 190 getting hits and a large piece of it falling off. Suddenly, he began to smoke, and I watched him fly by the cockpit going down. This attack happened in a matter of seconds.

"In the meantime, the Fw 190 had done a good job on us. I remember seeing the Plexiglas nose explode. Cannon shells had made a shambles of our cockpit instruments. Our No 2 engine was hit and windmilling. The radio compartment and bomb-bay had been destroyed. Our left gun position had been knocked out, leaving Sgt [Eugene H.] Buhler wounded. Cannon shells tore off a large chunk of our left rear stabilizer. Air streaming through our nose and the windmilling No 2 engine caused a severe drag on the airplane, which seemed to stop in mid-air."

With their aircraft crippled by this first fighter attack, the crew of *Ol' Dog* pulled on their parachutes and prepared to bail out. SSgt Norman H. Phillips was the radio operator:

Eighth Air Force gunners clean parts of their 0.50-in. Browning M-2 machine guns within the confines of a B-17G fuselage. Air gunners were drilled regularly over the importance of weapon maintenance, and after their first combat mission they would quickly come to learn that their lives depended on the reliability of their weapon. In this photograph, the barrels of the guns have been painted with their respective positions – *RADIO, R. CHIN, L. CHIN* and *L. NOSE.*

This view, from behind and above, shows a typical anti-B-17 formattion attack by a *Sturmgruppe*. The latter, comprising a *Stab* and three *Staffeln*, makes a massed, line-abreast (or in USAAF terms, a "Company Front") approach towards the bomber formation from behind. The escort to the Fw 190s – usually Bf 109s – can be seen flying above and behind the Fw 190s.

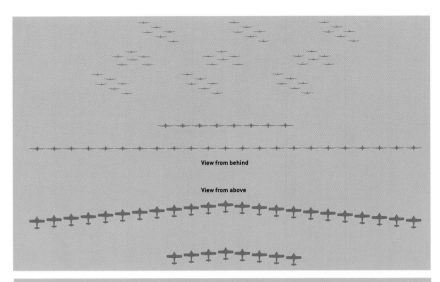

View from behind

View from above

View from behind

View from above

The attack formation breaks into three sections as it closes in with the B-17s, with each Fw 190 pilot theoretically targeting a bomber in the low, lead and high flights. The Fw 190s make their attack and pass through the formation, after which they would often reform for a second pass.

The Fw 190A-7, A-8 and A-9 variants were fitted with the Revi 16B reflector gunsight. This sight required the pilot to estimate the angle of deflection to the target according to combat conditions, but in reality, this was only possible with any degree of accuracy when engaging at short range and/or when attacking from a central position with minimum deflection. Thus, to shoot down a B-17 required considerable pilot skill. When attacking a Flying Fortress from either the side or behind – which would attract determined fire from its tail, top and ball turrets, as well as the waist guns – the pilot of a Fw 190 would have to remain equally determined and focused on his gunnery skills.

In a gunnery instruction document dealing with rear-mounted attacks on bombers of July 1944, German fighter pilots were instructed as follows:

"Your aircraft is your weapon. You must thoroughly master its capabilities. Not only your flying capability and correct tactical action, but also your mastery of the principles of gunnery and their practical application are vital to success.

"You must fire your weapons only at the ranges for which they were designed. Normally, you should not fire at ranges greater than 400m, as beyond this distance the trajectory quickly falls away. This also applies to larger weapons such as the MK 108. It is a common fallacy to believe that it must be possible to fire larger-caliber weapons at greater ranges, and that the aiming of these need not be as precise as for small-caliber weapons. The opposite is true! You have little ammunition! Use it sparingly. With the MK 108 you have only 60 rounds, so reduce range, aim carefully, fire accurately.

"Commence firing at a maximum range of 400m. Experience has shown that combat ranges are being greatly underestimated. The distances given in combat reports are almost never correct. When, for example, a combat range of 50–100 m is reported, it actually varies from between 200 and 400m, as established by analysis of combat films. Frequently, range estimation errors are even greater. In attacks against bombers, many fighters open fire at 2,500–3,000m. This is a senseless waste of ammunition!

"A four-engined bomber has a wingspan of about 30m. If it appears as large as the diameter of the deflection circle, it is at 300m range. For a four-engined bomber, the estimated value corresponding to a span of 30m is multiplied by three. Therefore, a four-engined bomber with 30m span fits in the circle one time – 1 × 3 = 300m; fits in the circle 2 times – 2 × 3 = 600m; fits in the circle 3 times – 3 × 3 = 900m.

"Learn this thoroughly and practice range estimation at every opportunity, then during combat you will no longer make gross errors."

"I was scared to death, and the thought of bailing out was distressing since it was the first time I had put on my 'chute without checking to see if the pin wasn't bent, which would cause it not to open."

Just as the emergency bell sounded – the signal to abandon the aircraft – word came over the intercom from the cockpit to defer bailing out, since the machine was still flyable. However, due to the constant drag caused by the wind rushing through the nose, a windmilling propeller and general battle damage, *Ol' Dog* fell behind its formation and found itself alone – a straggler, damaged and vulnerable, but still flying.

Eight members of the crew of B-17G Flying Fortress *Ol' Dog* of the 344th BS/95th BG are photographed in April 1945 whilst they were held as PoWs at Mooseburg. In the front row, from left to right, are Ralph Smithberger, George Reiff and Norman Ulrich. In the back row, again from left to right, are Rubin Schulman, Norman Phillips, Eugene Buhler, Leon Anderson and Norman Hines.

Ulrich dropped from 29,000ft to fly as low as possible so as to avoid flak and fighters. Then, after a unanimous decision by the crew to stay on board, a course was plotted towards neutral Sweden, the closest friendly territory. All surplus weight was jettisoned – guns, ammunition, flak suits, radio equipment, parachutes – even the ball turret was released.

"We got down to tree-top level", Ulrich remembered. "We couldn't have been any, more than 50ft above the ground. *Ol' Dog* was flying just fast enough so as not to stall out, and in a wobbly, haphazard way. I could see the leaves of the trees moving due to our prop wash, and I didn't think that we were going to stay airborne."

At around this time, two Fw 190s of IV.(*Sturm*)/JG 3 were returning to Salzwedel from their mission against the bombers. One of these was piloted by Unteroffizier Karl-Heinz Schmidt, who had joined *Sturmstaffel* 1 several weeks earlier. As of May 8, Schmidt had been credited with three victories. Approaching Salzwedel, he spotted the stricken B-17 and manoeuvred to intercept. Ulrich continued:

"It was about an hour after leaving the formation when we cleared a wood and found ourselves directly over a Luftwaffe airfield. SSgt [Leon E.] Anderson in the top turret opened fire on a green truck speeding along the perimeter track and I think he got it. Not long after leaving the airfield, someone hollered over the intercom that twin fighters were high and off to our front, carrying belly tanks. I wasn't sure what type of fighters they were, and I couldn't really see them at first. We figured they were US escort fighters, so I flew up to 1,500ft to show them who we were.

"When I gained height, the two fighters came roaring toward us. We realized that they were Fw 190s and I immediately dropped down to the deck so we wouldn't present such a fat target, and to allow our top turret guns to fire. The first Fw 190 came at us head-on, firing away. I thought he was going to come right through the pilot's window. Andy opened up on the approaching fighter from his turret. In a split second, cannon shells hit the turret, knocking Andy from it. He immediately fell on us in the cockpit, wounded and bleeding.

"The Fw 190 flew to the right of our cabin and over the wing. You could see him circling to come around for a second attack. I realized it was over at this point, with our only turret knocked out and with wounded aboard. I knew we were about to be shot down in flames, so I immediately ordered my co-pilot, George D. Reiff, to lower the landing gear as a sign of surrender.

"While all this was happening, the second Fw 190 was coming in for a side attack. At the last second he recognized that we were surrendering and waggled his wings, but not before buzzing our cockpit and veering off. He flew so close to our cabin that I thought I could touch him. As we flew on, the two Fw 190s circled us, and you could see them waving in their cockpits and we waved back."

This moment is borne out by one of Karl-Heinz Schmidt's former *Sturmstaffel* comrades, Oscar Boesch, who recalled:

"As Schmidt told the story, the B-17 was in bad shape, and he spotted it flying at a height of 500m above ground level. He intercepted it during his flight back to Salzwedel. Schmidt flew formation and signaled it to land. After some hesitation, it finally belly-landed into a farmer's field. After landing at Salzwedel, Schmidt drove out to the B-17 to extend 'welcome' greetings. It was still a gentleman's war."

As *Ol' Dog* dropped towards open fields near the small town of Packebusche, Ulrich instructed Reiff to raise the aircraft's wheels and cut the engines. But the American pilots knew there were still difficulties to overcome. The No 2 engine was still windmilling, the bomber felt nose heavy and the right wheel had not fully retracted.

Ulrich and his crew braced themselves for impact;

"As soon as we hit the ground, the No 2 engine broke off the engine nacelle and shot forward like a flaming rocket for several hundred yards. It was scary because we thought that the whole airplane was going to catch fire and explode. Gasoline was pouring out of fuel lines where No 2 had been. Before we could contemplate anything else, *Ol' Dog* came to a sudden and violent stop and stood vertically on her nose – we thought she was going flip over, but instead, she fell back flat on her belly. Thank God no one was in the nose. Andy was between George and me, and the rest of the crew was in the radio compartment.

"When *Ol' Dog* had stopped, I ordered everyone out of the airplane immediately. I looked out of my window and there was no fire to be seen. I could see the two Fw 190s circling above. For a split second I thought about getting a parachute and shooting it with a Verey pistol to destroy *Ol' Dog*, but I decided that we had to get the crew out of the airplane first. I ordered the crew not to attempt to escape, and to stay in the proximity of the airplane. I was concerned that if we tried to escape, the circling Fw 190s would open fire, killing us all."

One by one, the airmen scrambled out through *Ol' Dog*'s waist door and began to run from the aircraft, fearing that it would explode. As they did so, they noticed a group of curious civilians gathering to watch.

"It wasn't a mob as much as an excited group of old men and young boys", Ulrich recalled. "They were armed with antique shotguns, pre-World War I rifles, hoes, rakes

OVERLEAF
Major Walther Dahl, *Kommodore* of *Jagdgeschwader* 300, in his Fw 190A-8 Wk-Nr 170994 "Blue 13", and his wingman, Feldwebel Walter Loos, in "Blue 14", lead their *Gruppe* to attack the 39 B-17s of the 303rd BG over Bitburg as they make their way home from a mission to bomb Wiesbaden airfield on August 15, 1944. Dahl claimed his 74th victory – a B-17G north of Trier, some 45 minutes from the target on the return journey – at 1146 hrs, while Loos downed a second Fortress a minute later. The Fw 190s made their approach on the low group from high and to the rear, out of the sun, in a very "intense and fast developing" attack. It was the low formation of 13 B-17s from the 358th BS that took the brunt of the attack as the Fw 190s swept through the low-low echelon of three Fortresses, which included B-17G 44-6086 *My Blonde Baby*, piloted by 2Lt Oliver B. Larson. Its right wing exploded and broke away during the attack, and the aircraft crashed at Seffern. 2Lt John J. Draves was killed, but Lt Larson and the rest of his crew bailed out and were captured.

B-17G Flying Fortress *Ol' Dog* of the 344th BS/95th BG at its crash site near Packebusche on May 29, 1944. The bomber had been shot down by an Fw 190 flown by Unteroffizier Karl-Heinz Schmidt of IV.(*Sturm*)/ JG 3, who made a head-on attack. One of the B-17's crew recalled, "I thought he was going to come right through the pilot's window."

and sticks. The boys couldn't have been any older than 12. When the civilians reached us, the Fw 190s flew away. There was no animosity amongst this group toward us, and I believe this was the village of Packebusche's first glimpse of the war. They rounded us up and marched us into town. When we got into Packebusche, we were locked up."

Shortly after, a doctor arrived to tend to the wounded and injured airmen, and some local women brought linen, which they used as bandages. Then something unexpected happened, as Ulrich remembered:

"We heard a car drive up and then heard the doors shut. Four Luftwaffe men walked in. Two were dressed in blue uniforms and looked like officers. The other two were pilots, because they were wearing brown leather jackets and multi-pocketed flight pants. One of the men dressed in flight gear stepped out from the four and said, 'Who is the pilot?' I warily replied that it was me. His reaction wasn't what I expected. This fellow snapped his heels together and gave me a sharp, crisp salute, all the while extending his hand for a handshake. I shook his hand and he told me that he was the pilot who shot us down. This Unteroffizier Schmidt told me that he would get three points for shooting down a four-engined bomber.

"I told him that I had an engine shot out over Leipzig, and that if he was honest, he should only take part of the credit. When I said this, Unteroffizier Schmidt turned his head to see if any of his comrades were listening. The conversation could be compared to two football players from opposing teams discussing the game. This man had no hatred towards me – he was just doing his job."

Subsequently promoted to *feldwebel*, Karl-Heinz Schmidt was hit by defensive fire whilst attacking B-24s on August 3, 1944. He is listed as missing in action.

STATISTICS AND ANALYSIS

Research by the USAAF revealed that from August to November 1942, tail attacks by German fighters were the rule against B-17s. However, from December 1942 to the end of January 1943, nose attacks predominated. In February and March 1943, beam attacks increased, while from April to June, tail attacks picked up, beam attacks decreased and the number of nose attacks remained constant. The period July–December 1943 was marked by a high percentage of tail attacks and a decrease in the proportion of nose attacks, while from January–May 1944, the proportion of tail attacks decreased from 51 percent (January) to 31 percent (May), while nose attacks increased (22 percent in January to 44 percent in May). Between July and September 1944, there was a drastic reduction in the number of attacks from the nose quadrant.

In the first recorded analysis covering the month of January 1943, 37 percent of attacks by fighters against heavy bombers were low and 63 percent high. The proportion of attacks from below increased irregularly until, in December, 54 percent of attacks were low and 46 percent high. From that month on, attacks from below ran at about 46 percent.

On the German side, single-engined fighter production increased steadily throughout the first seven months of 1943 from about 480 to 800 aircraft per month, and with repaired aircraft added, some 1,000 fighters were available monthly. By 1 July, there were approximately 800 single-engined fighters available for the daylight defense of the Reich and the West, but they were being depleted in a growing battle of attrition at a rate that was difficult to sustain. In July 1943, fighter aircraft losses (all fronts) stood at 31.2 percent, while the loss in single-engined fighter pilots (all fronts and all causes) in July stood at 330, or 16 percent – an increase of 84 pilots on

An Fw 190 closes in on a B-17 from above and behind ("7 o'clock high"). The bomber's inboard port side engine is already on fire and the aircraft appears to be at a low altitude, suggesting that it could be a "straggler" which has already been attacked and damaged. Once it had dropped out of its box formation, a solitary Fortress was highly vulnerable to attacks like this.

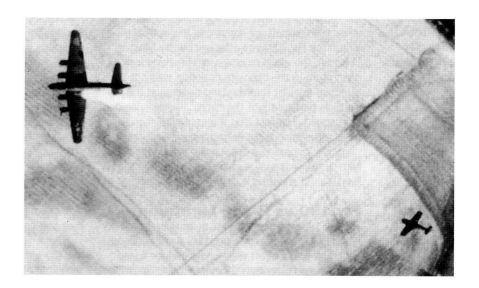

the previous month and of 64 more pilots than in May. Hard to bear was the accumulating loss of experienced fighter commanders.

In its summary for December 1943, I. *Jagdkorps* admitted "The numerically inferior German day fighter forces had succeeded neither in preventing a large-scale American attack nor in inflicting decisive losses on the enemy."

The ratio of total USAAF offensive effort in the operational area of I. *Jagdkorps* was 3-to-1 against German single- and twin-engined daylight fighter strength.

The pattern of American bombing throughout January 1944 was dictated to a great extent by the prevailing overcast weather over northwest Europe, which necessitated Pathfinder-led missions against German ports and industrial areas. The only major visual operation occurred on January 11, when the weather was expected to be fine. It was, however, to prove fickle, and the American bomber force of 663 aircraft pushed on in deteriorating conditions to hit several aviation and industrial targets in the heart of the Reich on a mission that was to mark the commencement of Operation *Pointblank* – the Allied strategic air offensive designed to bring about "the progressive destruction and dislocation of the German military and economic system".

The Luftwaffe was to put up the fiercest opposition since the second Schweinfurt raid on this day, although German fighters would fly only 239 sorties. By the end of the mission, the USAAF had lost 60 bombers – almost 11 percent of the total force – with one formation losing 19 per cent of its strength to enemy action. I. *Jagdkorps* reported 21 aircraft lost and a further 19 with more than 60 percent damage.

In February 1944, *Luftflotte Reich* stated that the numerical ratio was as as follows: "Total American strength (bombers and fighters) is 3.6. German single- and twin-engined fighter strength (I. *Jagdkorps*) is 1. American fighter strength is 1.6. German single- and twin-engined fighter strength (I. *Jagdkorps*) is 1."

I. *Jagdkorps* performed 2,861 fighter sorties in February, and losses in its area at the end of that month stood at 299 aircraft, or 10.3 percent of the total number of aircraft committed.

April brought little respite. On the 27th, during a month that had seen the loss of 489 pilots and the arrival of only 396 replacements, Adolf Galland warned industrialists, "The problem which the Americans have set the Jagdwaffe is quite simply the problem of air superiority. The situation is already beginning to be characterized by enemy mastery of the air. The numerical ratio in daylight operations is approximately 1:6 to 1:8. The enemy's standard of training is astonishingly high."

I. *Jagdkorps* calculated the following balance of forces for March and April 1944:

"Total American strength (bombers and fighters) March 1944 is 7.5. German total single- and twin-engined fighter strength (I. *Jagdkorps*) is 1. Total American strength (bombers and fighters) April 1944 is 4.5. German total single- and twin-engined fighter strength (I. *Jagdkorps*) is 1. American fighter strength March 1944 is 3.6. German single- and twin-engined fighter strength (I. *Jagdkorps*) is 1. American fighter strength April 1944 is 2.2. German single- and twin-engined fighter strength (I. *Jagdkorps*) is 1."

On May 15, Galland reported to Göring depressing average daily operational loss rates for the month of April – 38 percent in the area of *Luftflotte Reich*; 24 percent in *Luftflotte* 3; 18.2 percent in *Luftflotte* 2; 12 percent in *Luftflotte* 5; and 11 percent in *Luftlotten* 4, 6 and 1. In total, 489 fighter pilots had been lost in April, while reinforcements amounted to only 396.

A report prepared by the Operational Analysis Section at Headquarters, Eighth Air Force recorded that 398 bombers had been shot down by Luftwaffe fighters in March and April 1944, compared with 351 in the entire first 12 months of operations. Between April and November, losses to fighters averaged about 100 bombers per month. However, it was also recognized that since the acceleration and increase in the

B-17G 42-97391 *ANNIE McFANNIE* of the 427th BS/ 303rd BG is dowsed down by RAF fire crews, having made an emergency landing at Woodbridge airfield following a mission to Leipzig on June 28, 1944. Note the damage to one of the propellers on the starboard in-board engine. By the summer of 1944, an extremely high percentage of B-17s were succumbing to engine fires. 42-97391 was salvaged following this incident, having only been wih the 303rd BG since April 22.

scale of heavy bomber operations from early 1944, the true cost of attacks had decreased. From August 1942 to December 1943, fighters accounted for 4 percent of heavy bombers, while in the first half of 1944, losses decreased to 1.4 percent, and in the three subsequent months this figure averaged 0.5 percent. But it was noted that, "Except for the defensive measures against fighters adopted by us, the loss rate would probably have increased rather than decreased, because improved enemy fighter tactics made his attacks at least twice as lethal."

A survey of B-17 crews in the summer of 1944 revealed that between 75 and 85 percent of aircraft went down because of disabled engines, fire, explosions or an inability to feather the propellers.

Following the bitter summer of attrition and the Allied invasion of France, the OKL still saw the Jagdwaffe's prime mission in September 1944 as one of air defense and ensuring "domination of the air over friendly territory and the destruction of enemy aircraft by day and night". In reality, however, before "domination" could be achieved, a more immediate goal was "equality", and even on that count, the Jagdwaffe was substantially outgunned by Allied air strength by the autumn of 1944.

The emblem on the cowling of this Fw 190A-8 of *Stab*/JG 300 – a B-17 in the crosshairs of a gunsight – leaves little doubt as to the mission of its pilot. Just one Fw 190 of the unit is believed to have carried this emblem in very late 1944 – "Blue 13", assigned to *Jagdgeschwader Kommodore* Major Walther Dahl.

EIGHTH AIR FORCE HEAVY BOMBER LOSSES AUGUST 1942–SEPTEMBER 1944		
Period	Total Bombers Lost	Total Bombers Lost as Percentage of Attacking
5 months Aug–Dec 1942	31	4.0%
4 months Jan–Apr 1943	87	5.5%
4 months May–Aug 1943	369	6.4%
4 months Sep–Dec 1943	516	4.4%
2 months Jan–Feb 1944	425	3.5%
2 months Mar–Apr 1944	659	3.5%
2 months May–June 1944	540	1.4%
2 months July–Aug 1944	464	1.2%
1 month September 1944	248	1.6%

LEADING LUFTWAFFE B-17 KILLERS

	Unit(s)	Total Victory Claims	Heavy Bomber Victory Claims	B-17 Victory Claims
Major Georg-Peter Eder	JG 51, JG 2, JG 1, JG 26, *Kdo Nowotny*, EJG 2, JG 7	78	Est. 36	?
Major Anton Hackl	JG 77, JG 11, JG 76, JG 26, JG 300	192	Est. 34	?
Oberleutnant Konrad Bauer	JG 51, JG 3, JG 300	57	32	?
Oberstleutnant Walther Dahl	JG 3, JG z.b.v., JG 300, EJG 2	128	30	?
Oberstleutnant Egon Mayer	JG 2	102	26	21
Major Hermann Staiger	JG 20, JG 51, JG 26, JG 1, JG 7	63	25	Est. 21 + 3 HSS
Hauptmann Hugo Frey	LG 2, JG 1, JG 11	32	25	19
Hauptmann Hans Ehlers	JG 3, JG 1	55	24	18 + 3 HSS
Leutnant Alwin Doppler	JG 1, JG 11	29	25	16
Oberleutnant Werner Gerth	JG 53, *Sturmstaffel* 1, JG 3	27	22	16 + 1 HSS
Major Friedrich-Karl Müller	JG 53, JG 3	140	23	15
Hauptmann Hans Weik	JG 3, Erg.Gr.Ost, EJG 2	36	22	15 + 4 HSS
Oberfeldwebel Walter Loos	JG 3, JG 300, JG 301	38	22	?
Major Emil-Rudolf Schnoor	JG 1	32	18	15
Oberleutnant Adolf Glunz	JG 52, JG 26, EJG 2, JG 7	71	19	14 + 1 HSS
Major Hubert Huppertz	JG 51, JG 1, JG 5, JG 2	78	17	13
Leutnant Willi Unger	JG 3, JG 7	24	21	13 + 1 HSS
Leutnant Klaus Neumann	JG 51, JG 3, JG 7, JV 44	37	19	12 + 1 HSS
Oberfeldwebel Siegfried Zick	JG 11	31	18	12 + 1 HSS
Major Günther Specht	ZG 26, JG 1, JG 11	34	15	12
Oberstleutnant Heinz Bär	JG 51, JG 77, EJGr. Süd, JG 1, JG 3, EJG 2, JV 44	221	21	11 + 2 HSS
Oberleutnant Wilhelm Kientsch	JG 27	53	20	11 + 2 HSS
Major Erwin Clausen	LG 2, JG 77, JG 11	132	12	11
Hauptmann Harry Koch	JG 26, JG 1	30	13	10 + 3 HSS
Hauptmann Gerhard Sommer	JG 1, JG 11	20	14	4
Oberleutnant Franz Ruhl	JG 3	37	14	10 + 1 HSS
Oberst Walter Oseau	JG 51, JG 3, JG 2, JG 1	125	14	11
Oberfeldwebel Willi Maximowitz	*Sturmstaffel* 1, JG 3	27	15	10 + 2 HSS
Hauptmann Hans-Heinrich Koenig	ZG 76, NJG 3, *Jasta Helgoland*, JG 11	28	20	10 + 2 HSS

HSS – *Herausschuss*, or the separation of a bomber from its formation

AFTERMATH

From the early autumn of 1944, Allied fighters virtually ruled the skies over Germany. Losses amongst the *Jagdgeschwader* operating in the *Reichsverteidigung* were rising to nearly 30 percent, while victories gained amounted to less than 0.2 percent of Allied strength.

In the early hours of New Year's Day 1945, in a last-ditch attempt to strike back, the Luftwaffe launched a surprise low-level attack against 21 Allied airfields in northwest Europe. Codenamed Operation *Bodenplatte*, it had been conceived under great secrecy, and deployed 40 *Gruppen* drawn from ten *Jagdgeschwader*. It was a bold effort to mount such an operation at this stage of the war, and to the planners' credit it achieved significant surprise. It is believed that 388 Allied aircraft were destroyed or damaged. The effects, however, were grave. A total of 271 Bf 109s and Fw 190s were lost in the raid, with a further 65 damaged. Those aircraft shot down were largely flown at low level by young, poorly trained pilots who provided easy prey to Allied fighter pilots already airborne on early morning sorties.

Some 143 German pilots were killed or posted missing, with a further 21 wounded and 70 more captured. These figures included three *Geschwaderkommodore*, five *Gruppenkommandeur* and 14 *Staffelkapitäne*.

But the war against the bombers reached even more desperate heights. In March 1945 Göring asked for volunteers to take part in a radical operation "from which there is little possibility of returning". The plan was to assemble a group of pilots who would be prepared to fly their fighters in a massed attack against a large bomber formation using conventional armament, but also with the intent of ramming to bring the "heavies" down. From the initial call for volunteers, purportedly 2,000 pilots put their names forward to be available for the operation, which was to be codenamed *Wehrwolf*.

Many of the volunteers came from training units to be briefed by Oberfeldwebel Willi Maximowitz, a fearless pilot who had flown Fw 190s with *Sturmstaffel* 1 and IV.(*Sturm*)/JG 3, and who had shot down 15 *Viermots*. Further training included the showing of morale-boosting films and lectures on the dangers of Jewish culture and Bolshevism. Indeed, most of the training course consisted of political indoctrination, with only a small part devoted to tactics.

With favorable weather, and receipt of a codeword, the *Rammkommando 'Elbe'* was to approach the enemy formation at a height some 1,500m above the bombers. The approach was to consist of a long, shallow, dive, if possible out of the sun and in line astern. Fire was to be opened at extreme range and continued until the final steep ramming dive towards the fuselage of the bombers immediately forward of their tail units. If possible, the pilot was then to attempt to bail out. Combat with enemy fighters was to be avoided at all costs, and pilots were to climb away if attacked.

On April 7, 1945, 120 *'Elbe'* pilots took off with patriotic slogans broadcast into their headsets by a female voice. Their targets were the 1,261 B-17s and B-24s that had set out to bomb 16 targets across Germany that day. Immediately after the raid, however, the Eighth Air Force reported, "Signs of desperation are evidenced by the fact that Fw 190 pilots deliberately rammed the bombers, bailing out before their airplanes went into the bomber formations, and making fanatical attacks through a murderous

Mechanics take a break on the wing of an Fw 190A-7 of *Sturmstaffel* 1 at Salzwedel in late April 1944. The aircraft is fitted with a 300-liter drop tank, and has the unit's trademark spiral spinner and black-white-black fuselage band.

This B-17 of the 457th BG made it back home to Glatton despite having been struck by cannon fire in its port wing. A short burst from a pair of 30mm MK 108s was sufficient to "shred" the wing of a Fortress or Liberator.

hail of fire. Tactics were thrown to the wind. From today's reaction it would appear that although the enemy is fighting a losing battle, the German Air Force is preparing to fight to the finish in a fanatical and suicidal manner."

Seventeen bombers were lost, including at least five B-17s that appeared to have been rammed intentionally. In reality, the destruction of about 12 B-17s was attributable to *'Elbe'*, and some 40 German pilots were killed. This equates to a loss rate of 33 percent. It had been the last gasp.

American air power was unstoppable – and innovative. The YB-40 "gunship" had arrived in England in spring 1943, a purposefully heavily armed and armored variant of the B-17 that had been modified by Lockheed-Vega from an F-model. It fielded no fewer than 16 machine guns, and was designed to both escort bomber formations and draw the attention of enemy fighters. However, only 12 examples were built and delivered to the 327th BS/92nd BG, who used them on a number of missions between May and July 1943. Success was questionable, for the YB-40 suffered from poor flying characteristics at high altitude and in formation. And once the B-17s had dropped their bomb loads, the gunships struggled to keep up, as their bomb-bays were loaded with ammunition resulting in the YB-40 weighing in a ton heavier than an empty B-17F! The Eighth Air Force eventually abandoned them.

Experiments were also undertaken with war-weary B-17s packed with explosive and used as remotely controlled bombs, special H2X ground-scanning radar sets were trialed for poor weather operations, RAF Coastal Command flew Fortresses equipped with submarine-detecting radar in the anti-U-boat role and the Royal Canadian Air Force used them as transports in limited numbers. After the war, B-17 radio-controlled "drones" were used in the Bikini Atoll atom bomb tests of 1946–47 to provide data on blast and radiation, while limited numbers saw service with the newly formed state of Israel, as well as with the air arms of Dominica, Bolivia, Chile, Brazil and Portugal.

FURTHER READING

Bowman, Martin W., *Castles in the Air – The Story of the B-17 Flying Fortress Crews of the US Eighth Air Force* (Patrick Stephens, Wellingborough, 1984)

Bowman, Martin W., *Osprey Combat Aircraft 18 – B-17 Flying Fortress Units of the Eighth Air Force (Part 1)* (Osprey Publishing, Oxford, 2000)

Buckley, John, *Air Power in the Age of Total War* (UCL Press, London, 1999)

Budiansky, Stephen *Air Power – From Kitty Hawk to Gulf War II: A History of the People, Ideas and Machines that Transformed War in the Century of Flight* (Penguin Viking, London, 2003)

Caldwell, Donald, *The JG 26 War Diary Volume One 1939–1942* (Grub Street, London, 1996)

Caldwell, Donald and Richard Muller, *The Luftwaffe over Germany – Defence of the Reich* (Greenhill Books, London, 2007)

Campbell, Jerry L., *Focke-Wulf Fw 190 in Action* (Squadron/Signal Publications, Warren, 1975)

Carlsen, Sven and Michael Meyer, *Die Flugzeugführer-Ausbildung der Deutschen Luftwaffe 1935–1945 Band II* (Heinz Nickel Verlag, Zweibrücken, 2000)

Clarke, R. M.(ed), *Boeing B-17 and B-29 Fortress and Superfortress Portfolio* (Brooklands Books, Cobham, 1986)

Craven, W. F. and J. L. Cate, *The Army Air Forces in World War II, Volume I – Plans and Early Operations (January 1939 to August 1942)* (The University of Chicago Press, Chicago, 1948)

Forsyth, Robert, *Jagdwaffe – Defending the Reich 1943–1944* (Classic Publications, Hersham, 2004)

Forsyth, Robert, *Jagdwaffe – Defending the Reich 1944–1945* (Classic Publications, Hersham, 2005)

Freeman, Roger, *American Bombers of World War Two – Volume One* (Hylton Lacy Publishers, Windsor, 1973)

Freeman, Roger, *The U.S. Strategic Bomber* (Macdonald and Jane's, London, 1975)

Freeman, Roger, *B-17 Flying Fortress* (Janes, London, 1983)

Freeman, Roger A., *Mighty Eighth War Manual* (Janes, London, 1984)

Gobrecht, Lt Col (USAF Ret), Harry D., *Might in Flight – Daily Diary of the Eighth Air Force's Hell's Angels – 303rd Bombardment Group (H)* (The 303rd Bombardment Group (H) Association, Inc., San Clemente, 1993)

Hammel, Eric, *Air War Europa – America's Air War against Germany in Europe and North Africa: Chronology 1942–1945* (Pacifica Press, 1994)

Jablonski, Edward, *Flying Fortress – The Illustrated Biography of the B-17s and the Men Who Flew Them* (Purnell Book Services, London, 1965)

Lorant, Jean-Yves and Jean-Bernard Frappé, *Le Focke Wulf 190* (Éditions Larivière, Paris, 1981)

Lorant, Jean-Yves and Richard Goyat, *Jagdgeschwader 300 "Wilde Sau" – A Chronicle of a Fighter Geschwader in the Battle for Germany: Volume One June 1943–September 1944* (Eagle Editions, Hamilton, 2005)

Lorant, Jean-Yves and Richard Goyat, *Jagdgeschwader 300 "Wilde Sau" – A Chronicle of a Fighter Geschwader in the Battle for Germany: Volume Two September 1944–May 1945* (Eagle Editions, Hamilton, 2007)

Lowe, Malcolm V., *Osprey Production Line to Frontline 5 – Focke-Wulf Fw 190* (Osprey Publishing, Oxford, 2003)

McFarland, Stephen L. and Wesley Newton Phillips, *To Command the Sky – The Battle for Air Superiority over Germany, 1942–1944* (Smithsonian Institution Press, Washington, 1991)

Mombeek, Eric with Robert Forsyth and Eddie J. Creek, *Sturmstaffel 1 – Reich Defence 1943–1944 The War Diary* (Classic Publications, Crowborough, 1999)

Prien, Jochen, *IV./Jagdgeschwader 3 – Chronik einer Jagdgruppe 1943–1945* (strube-druck, Eutin, undated)

Rodeike, Peter, *Focke Wulf Jagdflugzeug Fw 190 A, Fw 190 "Dora", Ta 152 H* (strube-druck, Eutin, undated)

Unknown, *Target: Germany – The U.S. Army Air Forces' Official Story of the VIII Bomber Command's First Year over Europe* (HMSO, London, 1944)

Wadman, David and Martin Pegg, *Luftwaffe Colours Volume Four, Section 1, Jagdwaffe – Holding the West 1941–1943* (Classic Publications, Hersham, 2003)

OTHER RESOURCES

www.303rdbg.com

Correspondence with Willi Unger (1990)

Interview and correspondence with Oscar Boesch (1990)

Correspondence with Richard Franz (1991)

UKNA/AIR22/81 AMWIS *The New GAF Fying Training Policy*

US Strategic Bombing Survey, *The Impact of the Allied Air Effort on the German Air Force Program for Training Day Fighter Pilots 1939-1945*, USAFHRC Maxwell AFB

ADI(K) Report No. 334/1944: Some Notes on the Output and Training of GAF Fighter Pilots, July 6, 1944

ADI(K) Report No. 553/1944: The New GAF Flying Training Policy, October 10, 1944

Headquarters, Eighth Air Force, Operational Analysis Section, *An Evaluation of Defensive Measures Taken to Protect Heavy Bombers from Loss and Damage since the Beginning of Operations in the European Theater*, November 1944

Archiv: Journal of the International Society of German Aviation Historians – Gruppe 66, Vol. 3 No. 10 Ian Primmer: *Walther Dahl – Jagdflieger*

Gray, John M., *Old Dog's Last Flight*, National Museum of the United States Air Force *Friends Journal*, Vol. 16 No. 1, Spring 1993

Missing Air Crew Reports and associated papers for May 29, 1944

INDEX